ILLUMIN8

8 weeks
8 lessons
8 truths

Straight Talk for Street Smart Teens

ROBERT COOK

Straight Street Books
Lighthouse Publishing of the Carolinas

ILLUMIN8: STRAIGHT TALK FOR STREET SMART KIDS by ROBERT COOK
Published by Straight Street Books, an imprint of
Lighthouse Publishing of the Carolinas
2333 Barton Oaks Dr., Raleigh, NC, 27614

ISBN: 978-1-938499-21-0
Copyright © 2016 by Robert Cook
Cover design by: Ken Raney
Interior design by: Karthick Srinivasan

Available in print from your local bookstore, online, or from the publisher at:
www.lighthousepublishingofthecarolinas.com.

For more information on this book and the author visit: www.robcookunderground.com.

Brought to you by the creative team at Lighthouse Publishing of the Carolinas: Kevin Spencer,
Eddie Jones, Cindy Sproles, and Shonda Savage.

Library of Congress Cataloging-in-Publication Data
Cook, Robert
Illumin8: Straight Talk for Street Smart Teens/Robert Cook 1st ed.

Printed in the United States of America

This is a great book for teens, and adults as well. It's great for a quick read, or for reading piece by piece. It's directed at the reader. From the first page, you don't want to stop reading it. With the plain and simple way it's written, it's as if you're talking face-to-face with the author.

Ryan (19)

I am a youth leader for a church youth group. I had tried finding ways to relate to these kids through teaching but at times found it difficult to reach them and hold their interest. I stumbled across Regener8 and figured I would read it to see if it could provide some insight. I have been teaching using these devotionals as a curriculum for the past few weeks, and the results have been great. I highly recommend this devotional either for leaders or teenagers that are living in the reality of today's society.

Will
Youth Pastor

Our family loves this book! We are in the 7th week, and our sons are really engaged, asking many questions. We love the quality time it gives us, as well as the insight we as parents are receiving. Totally recommend this devotional for any family that has pre-teens and/or teens in it. I needed something for my 14 yr. old twin boys for a devotional that would not only help them in their difficult teens but be interesting. Regener8 really fit that need. They loved it. They were going to only read one a day, but had to finish it, and now are re-reading it. This book is very down to earth and speaks to what is important to teens. It challenges them to do the right thing. Thank you for this book!

Ruth

I can personally say that every parent needs this book for their sons. It is very relevant for today's teen generation. They are inundated with so much peer pressure, identity issues, and adult problems that teens should not have to face. Talking to parents is difficult enough, but to add topics that some parents shy away from, this book would really help as a tool to open the doors of communication. Boys in general do not share their emotions or problems unless they have a good mentor to talk to. This book opens dialogue that every parent and youth worker can easily discuss without it being uncomfortable. Rob Cook has been down many tough roads in his life which allows him to identify with young people. Because of this, doors have opened for him to really minister to broken teens who are hurting, in pain, and in crisis. To parents who have teens in crisis, this is a valuable resource. I urge you to get your copy today.

Stacy
Mother

This book is great for both parents and teens. Topics are broken down for easy reading, and all of the topics are relevant in today's world. It's not always easy for parents and kids to talk about some of these things, but this book gives you a starting point for conversation. It gives you a lot to think about as well. I highly recommend that you check it out. :)

Mercedes
Mother

Contents

At the end of each day, you will find a **Scripture Minute**. This is designed to help you become more familiar with the day's topic and the Word of God.

Foreword

I met Rob Cook at the Colorado Christian Writer's Conference when the director, a good friend, emailed me to tell me he and I were kindred spirits and had to hook up. I wasn't planning on making it to the conference that year, but trusted her that this was important so I made the two-hour drive from Denver to meet him. I thought, "What am I doing? If I'm lucky, this keynote speaker will give me 20-30 minutes of his time, and then he'll be off to play big-shot-cool-speaker-guy with all the wannabe writers clamoring for his attention. So I'm driving four hours for this?" Turns out, that's not how Rob is. We spent the entire afternoon together, and then I stayed on for his talk that evening. What I found in Rob is so Jesus, refreshing in this world where writers preach one word and live another.

Before I listen to what anyone has to say these days, I look at how they live. Jesus said He would be the Good Shepherd, and then was. He provided a living example of everything He taught, and so does Rob Cook. He's sacrificed a very lucrative career, and no doubt family and personal time, to serve young people looking for love—the very ones he's so powerfully written Illumin8 for. This devotional, at the same time, pierces your heart with adult insight and leaves you chuckling in the wake of youthful lingo and humor. You can tell Rob's been there. He writes the message so effectively because he's lived this message. And that's why it will reach out and touch you. This is a must read for young people looking for love, and adults trying to understand them.

Mike Wolff
Director: Reconnections Ministries
www.Thereconnectedchurch.org
A heart for men, and a calling to shepherd

Introduction

I know what you're thinking, *another boring church book my mom wants me to read.* Wrong.

Let your mom buy her own book. This book is just for you, for the stuff you wonder about: *Is the Devil even real? And what's with the pitchfork? How can sin look so good but be so bad? What's with Justin Bieber?* Okay, maybe not.

My name's Rob, and I'm just a regular dude who wrote a book called REGENER8 and told teens the truth about a lot of things adults normally don't.

I started getting teens, like you, contacting me about stuff. They knew I'd tell them the truth. No sugar-coating.

So that's what this book is about—answering your questions.

I figure you fall into one of two groups:

If you are in group one, you don't know much about God, Jesus, religion or why you still need to learn math when we have calculators. You are testing the waters to see what this Christianity thing is about. If this is you, come on in, the water's fine.

If you are in group two, at some point you probably went to some church youth event and some hip looking guy told you about some dude named Jesus who traveled around the desert spreading peace and love (way before The Grateful Dead).

He told you about this feel-good place called Heaven and a not-so-groovy hot place called Hell. He probably rambled on and told you that if you got hit by a bus on your way home from the church without accepting Jesus, you'd go directly to Hell, do not pass go. Do not collect $200.00

So you did whatever any sensible person would do under this kind of pressure. You checked to make sure everyone's heads were bowed, and eyes were closed, and then you quickly slipped your hand up and nabbed your get-out-of-Hell-free card. Yeah, Jesus!

Sorry to interrupt your victory dance—or whatever that was you were doing—but if you haven't yet figured this out, there is so much more to following Jesus than just escaping Hell.

ILLUMIN8 will shed some light on things like how the Devil operates, growing strong in your spirit, and getting closer to God. Don't worry, there are no math questions.

~ Rob

The Devil Has a Plan
for Your Life

ILLUMIN8

Week 1 Day 1

Illuminate

To provide or brighten with light (in this case, the Light of Truth). To enlighten intellectually or spiritually.

Where's the light switch?

If you are like me when I was young, you probably leave things laying around on the floor of your bedroom. For you, this may not pose a problem, but if you had lived in my house, it would have been a different story. At least at night.

My lamp was on my nightstand, which was the most logical spot for it since I liked to read at night before bed.

Here's the illogical part

There was no light fixture in the ceiling, and the light switch did not work the outlet my light was plugged into. This caused me to stumble through the dark to make my way over to my lamp. Here is where the problem was. If I had things haphazardly spread across my floor, I tripped or stubbed my toe, or worse, I stepped on something extremely hard or sharp in my bare feet.

You can't fix stupid

I've heard it said, the definition of stupid is doing the same thing over and over again and expecting a different result. If this is true, I was the poster child for STUPID. Each time I thought I could navigate the debris on my bedroom floor flawlessly and turn on my lamp unscathed. Every time, I was proven wrong.

Adjust to the dark ... not

I cannot count the times I said to myself I should buy a flashlight and leave it by the door. It's not like they were expensive. I could have bought one for five bucks. But each time, I convinced myself I didn't need it. I'd tell myself I'd just keep my room clean. I convinced myself my eyes would adjust to the dark and gave myself many reasons why I didn't need the light. But, in reality, I was living in denial.

Darkness is the absence of light. Without a flashlight, I'd fall over the things in my way. Without the light of the Gospel, we fall over the things that Satan places in the dark before us.

Five Minutes Equals Less Pain

Just like five bucks spent on a flashlight would light my path and guide me around the obstacles waiting to befall me, five minutes a day spent in God's word will lighten the path in front of you and expose the traps Satan is setting for you.

Daily Ammo

But everything exposed by the light becomes visible, for it is the light that makes everything visible. (Ephesians 5:13-14, NIV)

Scripture Minute

"This is the judgment, that the Light has come into the world, and men loved the darkness rather than the Light, for their deeds were evil. For everyone who does evil hates the Light, and does not come to the Light for fear that his deeds will be exposed. "But he who practices the truth comes to the Light, so that his deeds may be manifested as having been wrought in God."

(John 3:19-21, NAS)

Stop trippin'

Week 1 Day 2

Would You Like Filet Mignon With That?

If I offered to take you to dinner and gave you the choice of either eating at Outback Steakhouse or Burger King, most of you would choose Outback for obvious reasons. Better quality food, atmosphere, a 20oz. New York strip steak, etc.

But what if I took you to Burger King, and after you filled up on a Whopper and fries, I said, "Hey, would you rather go to Outback Steakhouse?" You'd probably be pretty upset. You'd wonder why I did not suggest Outback first.

You're too full now to enjoy a thick, juicy steak and baked potato. Forget about the Blooming Onion.

As you were enjoying your Whopper, you would have been content and happy. You would have been thinking wonderful thoughts about me for treating you to dinner.

Only when you found out about what you could have had, would you become upset. You'd start to regret the Whopper and crisp golden fries. The food might begin to feel like a lead weight in your stomach. How could something that seemed so good at the time seem so bad now? What's the difference?

Knowledge

Knowing what you sacrificed for that Whopper and fries. The knowledge of what you could have had. The image of the sizzling steak and steaming baked potato topped with piles of bacon smothered in cheddar cheese is overwhelming.

You wish you could turn back time, take a do-over, a mulligan. But you can't. No matter how much you want that steak there is just no room in your stomach for it.

Hungry as A Hostage

To truly enjoy a meal at Outback Steakhouse, you need to be hungry. You need to have an empty stomach. You don't eat at home before you go out to eat, at least not if you are smart. But there have been occasions where I went to my mom's for dinner and upon my arrival, was tempted by some triple chocolate cake she had baked. I'd take a big chunk against my mother's sound advice: "You won't have room for supper, wait."

I always assure her I'm so hungry it won't ruin my appetite. Guess who's always right? I argue my point: I never have room for dessert after dinner, so I'll eat dessert first. And don't act like you've never used that line before 'cause we both know you have.

Being tempted by the cake is not the problem. The problem starts when I don't resist the temptation and when I start reasoning with myself. I convince myself it won't hinder my ability to eat the dinner my mother went to the trouble of preparing for me.

The same thing happens when I go to Olive Garden. Those evil people bring me a big bowl of salad and that little wicker basket filled with piping hot, buttery breadsticks nestled in that crisp white linen blanket.

I eat three plates of salad and four breadsticks while I'm waiting for my Italian Trio of goodness to come. But then the waitress comes and asks, "Would you like some more salad and breadsticks?" And she is so polite, I don't want to say no and hurt her feelings, so I thoughtfully say, "Absolutely." I mean what am I supposed to say?

Two more plates of salad and three breadsticks later, I can't move. Right on cue, my trio of chicken parmesan, lasagna, and fettuccini Alfredo arrives. The waitress smiles and asks, "Can I get you anything else?" I'm like yeah, a to-go box because I'm stuffed. You can't eat a loaf of bread and two heads of lettuce and expect to polish off a boat-sized plate of pasta. Your stomach needs to be empty.

What's My Point?

So you may be wondering, *is there some Bible message in all this?*

Actually, believe it or not, there is. Sure, there is the part about temptation, but there is more to today's message than the evils of being tempted. It's about being filled up with the wrong stuff. It's about not having any room for the right stuff.

When Satan was tempting Jesus with food, Jesus was able to resist because he was already full.

Jesus answered, "It is written: 'Man does not live by bread alone, but on every word that comes from the mouth of God.'" (Matthew 4:4, NIV)

Jesus was quoting Old Testament scripture. He was filled with God's word. Jesus filled himself with the things of his Father.

Knowledge of the scriptures gave Jesus the ability to resist the Devil.

Food For Thought

I have hidden your word in my heart that I might not sin against you. (Psalm 119:11, NIV)

Scripture Minute

*Above all else, guard your heart, for it is
the wellspring of life.*

(Proverbs 4:23, NIV)

For as he thinks in his heart, so is he.

(Proverbs 23:7, NKJV)

A man reaps what he sows.

(Galatians 6:7, NIV)

*You brood of vipers, how can you who are evil
say anything good?
For the mouth speaks what the heart is full of.*

(Matthew 12:34, NIV)

*But the things that come out of the mouth come from the heart, and
these make a man 'unclean.' For out of the heart come evil thoughts,
murder, adultery, sexual immorality, theft, false testimony, slander.*

(Matthew 15:18, 19, NIV)

*That if you confess with your mouth, "Jesus is Lord," and believe in
your heart that God raised him from the dead, you will be saved.
For it is with your heart that you believe and are justified, and it is
with your mouth that you confess and are saved.*

(Romans 10:9, NIV)

Don't spoil your appetite

Week 1 Day 3

Get Out Your #2 Pencils

We all know what that means … a test. I don't know about you, the only test I like is an open-book test. Those are always easy for me because the answers are right in front of me. It's a no-brainer.

In Matthew Chapter 4, we see that Jesus was tested as well:

"Then Jesus was led by the Spirit into the desert to be tempted by the DEVIL." (And you thought you had it rough.) *"After fasting forty days and forty nights, he was hungry. The tempter came to him and said, 'If you are the Son of God, tell these stones to become bread"* (Matthew 4:4, NIV).

Time to Make the Donuts

I don't know about you, but I'd be putting on an apron and baking me some bread. Not Jesus. He knew the right answer. If you were paying attention yesterday, so do you.

Jesus answered, "It is written; 'Man does not live on bread alone, but on every word that comes from the mouth of God.'"

Then the Devil took him to the holy city and had him stand on the highest point of the temple. "If you are the Son of God," he said, "throw yourself down. For it is written: 'He will command his angels concerning you, and they will lift you up in their hands, so that you will not strike your foot against a stone.'"

(I'd be like, in your face Satan, and I'd swan dive into the angel's arms. Not Jesus. Again, he knew the right answer.)

Jesus answered him, "It is also written: 'Do not put the Lord your God to the test.'"

Again, the Devil took him to a very high mountain and showed him all the kingdoms of the world and their splendor. "All this I give to you," he said, "if you will bow down and worship me."

(Jesus had had enough of Satan's nonsense.)

Jesus said to him, "Away from me Satan! For it is written: 'Worship the Lord your God and serve him only.'"

Then the Devil left him, and the angels came and attended him. (Matthew 4:4-11, NIV)

Method to His madness

The Devil did not come to Jesus in his moment of strength. Like when Jesus was being baptised and his Father, God, was praising him. Like when the Holy Spirit was floating down on him like a dove.

The Devil knew he had no chance of getting Jesus to sin. Satan knew Jesus would not fall for his tricks. Not when he was so close to his Father. He waited for Jesus to be at his weakest moment, his lowest point.

It's important to note that when Satan was tempting Jesus, he quoted scripture. He has fooled many people with this technique.

Satan means well, right?

Just imagine if you had not eaten for 40 days and 40 nights. We can't even go 40 minutes sometimes without snacking. Imagine roaming in the heat of the barren, hostile desert without food for over a month. Your body, frail and exhausted, every step a monumental effort. Your mind unable to think straight. Your laser focus: GET FOOD NOW!

That's when Chef Satan makes his move. That's when he puts out the spread, the all-you-can-eat buffet: prime rib, mashed potatoes and gravy, fried chicken, macaroni and cheese, baked lasagna, and roast beef. Just the smell of the savory aroma causes you to salivate. Plus an entire table of cakes and pies?

You would do anything to devour this delectable smorgasbord of awesomeness. I'm getting hungry just writing about it, and I just had lunch 20 minutes ago.

This is when Satan knows he has a chance of snaring you. When you are weak and starving, craving sustenance, broken and alone. He will bring all the things YOU think YOU need to restore yourself.

How can this be bad, right? It's only food. It smells so good, and you are starving. Satan is just trying to help … right? Maybe he ain't so bad after all. People have just misunderstood him. They've been misinformed.

Before you know it, you're caught up in his trap. Only after you have put your trust in him, do you find the food is rotting and full of maggots.

How was Jesus able to resist the temptation? How did he not fall for it? Jesus did not fall into Satan's trap because he was close to the Father through His word. Jesus used scripture to counter Satan's attack. Jesus has hidden the Word in his heart. To him, it was an open-book test. He had memorized the answers. A test is always easier when you are prepared.

Do your best to present yourself to God as one approved, a workman who does not need to be ashamed and who correctly handles the word of truth (2 Timothy 2:15, NIV).

Scripture Minute

The brethren immediately sent Paul and Silas away by night to Berea, and when they arrived, they went into the synagogue of the Jews. Now these were more noble-minded than those in Thessalonica, for they received the word with great eagerness, examining the Scriptures daily to see whether these things were so. Therefore many of them believed, along with a number of prominent Greek women and men.

(Acts 17:10-12, NAS)

Don't give the devil an inch
He will become your ruler

Week 1 Day 4

Counterfeit Benjamin

I went to the bank once with a friend so he could cash his check, and then we stopped by a store so he could get a few things. When it came time to pay for his goods, he handed the cashier a hundred-dollar bill. She rubbed her fingers over it and made a face. It was not a good face.

She proceeded to hold it up in the light. She turned it over and over in her hands. She studied that bill like there was going to be a test. She even sniffed it.

My buddy asked if there was something wrong. She informed him the bill was counterfeit. We didn't believe it. My friend objected and told her he had just gotten the hundred from a bank, so there was no way it was counterfeit.

That's when she brought out her marker and settled things. It was indeed fake.

Schooled

My friend was incredulous, and I have to admit, so was I. How could this convenience store clerk spot a fake hundred-dollar bill when a bank teller could not?

Aren't bank tellers like professional money-handlers or something? They are around money all day. Shouldn't they be the first ones to spot a counterfeit?

McDonald's sends their employees to Hamburger University to learn how to put a slab of beef between two pieces of bread. Shouldn't tellers have to go to Phony Money University or the College of the Real McCoy? I mean seriously, right?

I had to know what made her the qualified queen of counterfeit cash. She proceeded to explain that she had worked for her father at his store when she was younger. Her father worked many hours to make ends meet, but they still struggled. Occasionally, she would get hit with a counterfeit bill, and her father would become upset with her.

She became determined that it would never happen to her again and studied the bad bills religiously. The feel of the texture of the paper. The color of the ink. The way light shone through the paper. In time, she could tell a bill was counterfeit the second it was placed in her hands.

She proudly proclaimed, "I never got stuck with a bad bill again." Too bad my friend could not say the same.

So it got me to thinking

How come the bank teller was not just as passionate as Sally (we learned her name) was about spotting counterfeit money?

This is the conclusion I came up with: Sally had a personal stake in the ability to determine if a bill was fake or not. If she continued to be fooled by the bad bills, her family's business would suffer, her father would be disappointed with her, and she could lose her job. Learning how to spot phony money directly benefited her.

But, more importantly, she had made a decision, she had taken a stand. This was never again going to happen to her. She would be the Victor, not the Victim. She not only made that declaration, but she followed it up with action. She took the steps necessary to learn everything she could about spotting fakes. She told us she spent quite a bit of time studying and examining real money. In fact, she shared with us that she had spent considerably more time studying the genuine article. She told me when you are well acquainted with the real thing, it's easier to spot the fakes.

Imposters

False teachers are as worthless as fake money. The trick is knowing when someone is attempting to deceive you. But is it really a trick? Was Sally's discovery of the counterfeit one-hundred-dollar bill a trick?

Sally had taken the necessary steps to become an expert in the field of counterfeit money. Being informed is not a trick. Knowing what to look for is the key to success. An intimate understanding of the genuine article hinders an imposter's ability to deceive you

What big teeth you have, Granny

I'm sure you've heard the fairy tale of Little Red Riding Hood. The wolf eats granny, slips into her pajamas and jumps into bed. In the story, Red sees right through the costume, but that is not always the case in real life.

The writer, Luke, in the Book of Acts warns us:

I know that after I leave, savage wolves will come in among you and will not spare the flock. Even from your own number men will arise and distort the truth in order to draw away the disciples after them. So be on guard! (Acts 20:29-31, NIV)

And Jesus warned, *"Watch out for false prophets. They come to you in sheep's clothing,"* (or dressed as granny), *"but inwardly they are ferocious wolves."* (Matthew 7:15, NIV) The wolf in the fairy tale was easy to spot. He had more hair than granny. More teeth than granny. And he had big feet. But how are we supposed to spot the wolves?

Red Riding Hood knew the answer. She knew what her real granny looked like.

Scripture Minute

For such people are false apostles, deceitful workers,
masquerading as apostles of Christ. And no wonder, for Satan
himself masquerades as an angel of light. It is not surprising, then, if
his servants also masquerade as servants of righteousness. Their end
will be what their actions deserve.

(2 Corinthians 11:13-15, NIV)

Dear friends, do not believe every spirit, but test the spirits to see
whether they are from God, because many false prophets have gone
out into the world.

(1 John 4:1, NIV)

Know what the real Jesus looks like.

Week 1 Day 5

Marketing Guru

So Eve was the first one to ever market a product. Even though she was just a beginner, she had the secret of selling down pat, because Satan was her sales coach.

Here's the scene:

Adam's chillin' and he looks up from his video game and there, standing before him, is his perfect, beautiful … naked wife, and she's holding an apple pie.

Do you think he said to himself, *I'm not supposed to eat the apple, so I better say, no.*

Not a chance. He was too busy looking for the vanilla ice cream.

Satan used Eve, Adam's wife, to distract him from the truth. If Satan had come to Adam with his Halloween devil costume on and said, "Adam eat this apple so you will be forever separated from God, get kicked out of this sweet garden, and have to work hard every day for the rest of your life, and oh yeah, die."

What do you think Adam's response would have been? Certainly not, "Where's the whipped cream?"

Cracks In Your Armor

Satan knows your weakness. For guys, it just happens to be naked women holding pastry.

Satan does his homework. He studies our habits to interpret our thoughts. He analyzes our behavior and body language. He plays with possible scenarios and predicts possible outcomes. He is smart and cunning. His flawless strategy fells many.

He has been at this game for a long time. As a matter of fact, he invented it. Deception, Death, and Destruction. The original 3D game. The problem is … there are no winners, ever.

Winning!

Like every arch villain in every Marvel blockbuster, you may think you are winning but still be totally losing. It's like playing the game Chutes and Ladders. You start off great, you're cruising up the ladders, leaving everyone in the dust. You quickly find yourself all the way at the top.

Commence, Smack Talking

The finish line is in sight. Victory is within your grasp … then the bottom drops out, literally. You land on a slippery slide to the bottom. You are devastated. You never saw it coming. You just didn't think it could happen to you. You gambled with the odds and lost.

This is not a big deal. It's just a board game. (Okay, for me, it was.) It is, however, a big deal with terrible consequences in real life.

Coming to the end of your life, only to discover you have been tricked and deceived by Satan, is inconceivable.

One way Satan distracts you from the truth is by convincing you that being a good person is enough to earn a ticket to Heaven. Satan quoted scripture when he tried to tempt Jesus, and he uses religion today. Religion tells you all the things you should not do. It lists all the right things you are supposed to do.

Go to church. Give money. Be nice to people. We get conditioned that our actions are enough. We believe we will stand before God, and he will drag all our deeds onto a big scale. If the good stuff outweighs the bad, you're in.

Religion becomes man's attempt to appease God. This is Satan's best trick. He has used it millions of times for thousands of years.

Whenever you start to think maybe there just might be a problem, Satan points out your neighbor Joe and whispers, "Come on, you ain't as bad as him. Remember, you went to church last Sunday. Joe ain't ever been to church. And don't forget, you tossed five bucks into the offering plate last month."

You listen to the little voice and go on feeling pretty good about yourself.

I Never Knew You

Let's see what Jesus has to say about your "good deeds."

"Not everyone who says to me, 'Lord, Lord,' will enter the kingdom of

heaven, but only he who does the will of my Father who is in heaven. Many will say to me on that day, 'Lord, Lord, did we not prophesy in your name, and in your name drive out demons and perform many miracles?' Then I will tell them plainly, 'I never knew you. Away from me you evildoers!'" (Matthew 7:21-25, NIV)

Gives new meaning to the phrase, No good deed goes unpunished.

Be prepared

How do you get prepared? Read the Word. Satan has not changed his M.O. in ten thousand years. If you know how he rolls, you can shut him down.

Scripture Minute

All of us have become like one who is unclean, and all our righteous acts are like filthy rags; we all shrivel up like a leaf, and like the wind our sins sweep us away.

(Isaiah 64:6, NIV)

For it is by grace you have been saved, through faith—and this is not from yourselves, it is the gift of God—not by works, so that no one can boast.

(Ephesians 2:8-9, NIV)

I think my wife is baking apple pie. Gotta go!

Week 1 Day 6

What Forest?

I'm sure you have heard the expression, 'You can't see the forest for the trees.' For the benefit of those, who like me, had no idea what this meant:

We go on a trek to the top of Everest to ask the old man wrapped in a sheet, sporting a Gandalf beard, to enlighten us. Here is what he has to say; "If you can't see the forest for the trees, you can't see the whole situation clearly because you are looking too closely at small details, or because you are too closely involved."

No Texting during the movie

Here is a pet peeve of mine, and maybe one of yours as well. I'm sitting in a movie theater, gallon of soda on my right, jumbo Sno-caps in the cup holder to my left, and a dumpster of hot buttery popcorn in my lap. The lights go down, the screen does its little mechanical adjustment, so the movie fits just right, and I am in the zone. After what seems like two hours of previews, we are told to be courteous to others, and please silence your cell phones. We are also told not to text during the movie. For me, this is just common sense.

The movie starts, and I'm loving it, and then some inconsiderate dweeb in front of me whips out his cell phone and blinds me because it just happens to be the new Samsung something-or-other with the new HD 30-inch screen.

I'm immediately pulled out of the storyline and right into a new zone. It's called smash-his-phone zone. I try to relax and give him the benefit of the doubt. Maybe he has to check in with his pregnant wife who is in labor to see how far apart her contractions are. But he keeps texting, and my pulse is pounding, and my stomach has those little butterflies I get when I'm about to do something I know I shouldn't.

I lean forward to see if I can see what is so important that he cannot wait another 90 minutes. My rage blinds me to most of it, but, I see a lot of lols and OMGs and wuz ups to only add fuel to my fire. His wife is not in labor. His house is not burning down. He is just talking to a buddy about what they are going to do later. After about 15 minutes, he puts the phone away and goes on happily watching the movie.

Not me

I was so mad about the whole ordeal I could not concentrate on the screen. I had missed some key plot points while I was reading over his shoulder. I was angry at him for ruining my movie experience. He, on the other hand, was oblivious to what he had put me through. He seemed to have totally enjoyed the movie and talked lively about it with his buddies on the way out. He commented that it was the best movie he had ever seen. I grumbled to myself, "best movie I NEVER saw."

Driving home, I thought about how I missed the year's biggest picture because of that stupid phone … then I suddenly became reflective. I realized I had become so focused on the little thing that I missed the big picture, literally. I realized there was a lesson for me to learn.

Distractions, distractions

I thought of all the times God had big things in the works for the movie called, "My Life," and Satan distracted me with worries about finances or some other perceived problems. I would miss God's voice because Satan blinded me with my own smartphone. Status updates and tweets had taken precedence over quality time in the Word or communicating with my Father God.

Even being angry at the phone guy was a distraction in my walk with God. I had worked myself into a frenzy of evil thoughts about things I wanted to say and do to him. Ever been there? All you can think about is revenge. If not, good for you. I cannot say the same. But at that moment in my car, this verse came to mind:

"For if you forgive men when they sin against you, your heavenly Father will also forgive you. But if you do not forgive men their sins, your Father will not forgive your sins." (Matthew 6:14-15, NIV)

These words came straight from the mouth of Jesus. I could not ignore them. I forgave the phone guy and asked for forgiveness myself.

Scripture Minute

Be on your guard; stand firm in the faith;
be men of courage; be strong. Do everything in love.

(1 Corinthians 16:13-14, NIV)

Be self-controlled and alert.
Your enemy the devil prowls around like a roaring lion
looking for someone to devour.

(1 Peter 5:8, NIV)

Don't let Satan distract you with the little things.
In the eyes of God, everything is little.

Week 1 Day 7

1) What are some areas in your life where you feel the Devil is trying to build a stronghold? (A stronghold is _____ _____.)

2) When you are tempted by Satan, what are some things you can do to overcome the temptation?

3) What are some of the distractions in your life that hinder your relationship with God?

4) What are some action steps you could take to remove or lessen these distractions?

5) Is there anyone you are angry with or have a grudge against?

6) **What can you do on your part to rectify the situation with these people?**

Memorize:

For if you forgive men when they sin against you, your heavenly Father will also forgive you. But if you do not forgive men their sins, your Father will not forgive your sins. (Matthew 6:14-15, NIV)

**Bodybuilding for
Spiritual Growth**

Week 2 Day 1

Heart Muscle

Most people believe that working out, exercising, and lifting weights is not only healthy but beneficial to their overall quality of life. Whether or not they back that knowledge up with action is another story. The same is true for your spiritual health and well-being.

So we at least understand the value of developing our bodies. We go to school to develop our minds, but somehow we fail to see the benefits of developing our spiritual life.

Jesus understood the importance of spiritual development. He worked out his heart muscle. He had hidden God's word in his heart and was able to overcome Satan's temptations.

The Apostle Paul in his letter to Timothy gave this advice:

For physical training is of some value, but godliness has value for all things, holding promise for both the present life and the life to come. (1 Timothy 4:8, NIV)

Lose 30 pounds in 30 days

We have all seen colorful ads in magazines featuring before and after pictures of the amazing transformation of some guy or girl. All they did was take these magic pills. The before picture shows a pale, overweight person who looks miserable. The "after" picture does not even closely resemble the same person. Their muscles have muscles. They are tan. They are smiling. Their kegs have melted into six packs. All this from just swallowing 3 pills a day for 30 days.

I'm not saying the pills do not burn fat. I'm telling you with all certainty that popping some pills is not all the people did. Sure, the pill manufacturers would love for you to believe that, and they fool many people, but in reality, a lot of intense weight training went along with the pill consumption.

Burning fat will not give you rock hard muscles. Burning fat will not give you an all over tan. Exercise, along with a proper nutritional diet, will give you muscles. The fine print on the bottle will even tell you this information. The funny thing is, if you were eating healthy and exercising in the first place, working out would burn the fat and get you in shape.

Here's the point

Popping some fat burners will not make you healthy any more than attending church one day a week will keep you spiritually fit.

Quick-fix weight loss will not last if you do not develop a healthy lifestyle. There are many variables that go into maintaining a great physique.

Expecting to stay spiritually healthy from a pastor's message one day a week makes you as wrong as the guy who thinks he can go to the gym and get muscles by watching other people work out.

You must do the work

If you feed your body one day a week, you will be physically weak. If you feed your spirit once a week, you will be spiritually weak. Do the math.

You want to be strong? Exercise daily. You want to be spiritually strong, able to resist the Devil and his minions? Eat from the word of God daily. Chew it up. Devour it.

Scripture Minute

Jesus answered, "It is written: 'Man does not live on bread alone, but on every word that comes from the mouth of God.'"

(Matthew 4:4, NIV)

Blessed are those who hunger and thirst for righteousness, for they will be filled.

(Matthew 5:6, NIV)

Go eat your Bible

Week 2 Day 2

Armed and Dangerous

The Bible is a double-edged sword, and like any weapon, it's dangerous if not used properly. People can and will get hurt. A lot of well-meaning people read the Bible just enough to be dangerous, but not in a good way. Satan loves this fact because he does not have to do anything at all to turn people away from God. He just sits back and watches the show.

Say you wanted to own a gun. The smart and responsible thing to do would be to take training classes on the proper use of it. At a shooting range, you would learn how to safely handle a gun and learn how to shoot. You would also learn important maintenance techniques and how to properly store the gun.

Your instructor would tell you to always assume a gun is loaded. You would be told that after removing the clip, always clear the chamber.

Many people have been seriously injured or killed because someone thought they "knew" the gun was empty. The very thing that was meant to protect their life destroys their life.

The Bible Equals Loaded Gun

Just like a careless gun owner can destroy lives, so does a careless Bible reader. You may have met one at some point. One of them may have even kept you from making a decision to follow Christ. They read a few verses out of context and then run out with this new found "Truth" and fire into a crowd with the safety off. People are wounded. Spirits are killed. Satan loves when people misquote scripture.

Phantom Verses

Satan has a few tried and true favorite misquotes he loves; *God helps those who help themselves.* (Ben Franklin actually said this.) *Money is the root of all evil.* (It's the LOVE of money that is the root of all evil.) *God will never give you more than you can handle.* An *eye for an eye. Have nothing to do with unbelievers. God works in mysterious ways* (actually from English poet William Cowper). *Cleanliness is next to Godliness.* (John Wesley, 18ᵗʰ-century evangelist.)

The key to avoiding the "Art" of misquoting scripture is to avoid the way most people read the Bible, if they read it at all.

Here is how most people read the Bible. They say to God, "Show me what you want to tell me today." Then they randomly open the Bible and wherever they end up, that is obviously what God wants them to read. They start reading where their finger lands, usually in the middle of the text, so, therefore, everything is out of context because they have no reference as to what came before or after the few verses they read. After two or three minutes of "heavy" Bible study, they close the book and head out the door, wielding a dangerous weapon with the safety off.

They fire off this "knowledge" and alienate people with their "truth." When people get upset with them, it only strengthens their resolve because they remember reading somewhere that when you are a Christian, people will hate you—so they must be doing something right.

Peter warned against these people: *"...His, (Apostle Paul's), letters contain some things that are hard to understand, which ignorant and unstable people distort, as they do the other Scriptures, to their own destruction."* (2 Peter 3:16, NIV)

Thrift Store Theology

Another common problem is that many people who quote scripture have never even read the Bible. They go to church and get their theology from a pastor. I call this second-hand knowledge or hand-me-down theology.

If you are a second or third child in a family, you are familiar with hand-me-downs. You get "new" clothes when your older siblings are done with them. The clothing is not your own. It was meant for someone else. It may not fit right, but your mom tells you, "You'll grow into it." You want something of your own. You don't want second-hand goods.

I came from a single-parent home, and my mom struggled to make ends meet. When it came time to buy us new school clothes, she would go to the Goodwill thrift store and purchase and bring clothes home to us.

I don't know about you, but I like to shop for myself. I want to try on the clothes and see how I look in the mirror. I want to buy things I like. I like the whole experience.

I also like to be the first one wearing my clothes. I never want the display model. I want new in the box stuff. Having someone else read the Bible and then tell you how they think you should "wear" this knowledge in your life, robs you of the experience. Going to church is a fundamental part of spiritual development in addition to your own personal Bible study. But if this is all you are getting, it's like having someone chew your food for you then ram it down your beak, and that's for the birds.

Scripture Minute

All scripture is God-breathed and is useful for teaching, rebuking, correcting and training in righteousness, so that the man of God may be thoroughly equipped for every good work.

(2 Timothy 3:16-17, NIV)

For everything that was written in the past was written to teach us, so that through endurance and the encouragement of the Scriptures we might have hope.

(Romans 15:4, NIV)

Do not let this Book of the Law depart from your mouth; meditate on it day and night, so that you may be careful to do everything written in it. Then you will be prosperous and successful.

(Joshua 1:8, NIV)

Chew your own food, it tastes better

Week 2 Day 3

Practice makes perfect

The more you do something, the better you get, hopefully. I have met a few exceptions to this rule. But for the most part, this statement is true. Ask any great pitcher how many balls he threw before he stepped on that mound. The NBA star how many three-pointers he attempted in a back lot somewhere before he ever set one foot on those shiny boards. How many footballs the NFL kicker kicked before he was drafted.

By the time these stars play their first game in front of millions, they have already spent countless hours honing their skills. We watch in amazement at this "natural talent," convinced we could never do this.

We falsely come to this conclusion because we are looking at the finished product. We didn't see the thousands of hours of practice or the blood, sweat, and tears.

What do baseballs have to do with the Bible?

Good question. I'm glad you asked. The answer, nothing really, but then again it's just an analogy. For what? Another great question. I am impressed with your participation.

Undoubtedly, as you start to meet more Christians, you will meet the guy who spouts off Bible verses from memory. Not just a couple, but hundreds of them. He has a verse up his sleeve for every situation. He'll tell you the book where it's found and the verse number. He might even be able to tell you the page number.

This used to blow my mind. I thought these "freaks", were ... well, freaks. How in the world could they memorize all those verses? Didn't they have jobs? Families? A life? I just knew that I would never be able to memorize a bunch of verses. I just didn't have it in me ... or did I?

Radio Junkie

I had a pretty rough childhood and buried myself in music. It was my escape. I played records on my psychedelic colored record player every day and sang along with the radio at the top of my lungs in the shower. I carried my big boom box everywhere I went. I even tied it to the handlebars of my bicycle. It blared AC/DC, Quiet Riot, and Def Leppard. I memorized the lyrics to hundreds of songs … wait, what? I had memorized hundreds of songs? Thousands of words? How was this possible?

Repetition

DJs play the popular songs over and over. Sometimes they will play a hit every hour. The first time we hear it, we can't sing along. The second or third time, we are singing along, only to find out we have some of the words wrong. The tenth time we hear it, we sing it like we wrote it.

That, my friends, is how the "freak" does it. Yes, he has a job. Yes, he has a family and a life. But instead of filling his mind with junk, he spends time reading the Word of God every day. He reads some on his lunch break. He might listen to a CD of the Bible on the way to work. It's downloaded on his iPod. It's important to him.

You too can memorize scripture, just like you memorize the lyrics to your favorite songs.

Scripture Minute

Moses gave us this advice:
"These commandments that I give you today are to be upon your hearts. Impress them on your children. Talk about them when you sit at home and when you walk along the road, when you lie down and when you get up."

(Deuteronomy 6:6-7, NIV)

You can sing in the shower, just don't read your Bible in the shower.

Week 2 Day 4

Do you suffer from narcotizing dysfunction?

I recently joined a gym … again. Hopefully, this time I'll actually go. I always convince myself I will use my gym membership since I am paying good money for it, but somehow that does not relate to action.

In the months leading up to my joining the gym, I read several articles in Men's Health about the importance of exercise and proper diet. I researched and became well informed about the various workouts featured in Muscle & Fitness magazine. I wanted a certain result. I purchased all the vitamins they recommended. I'm good to go.

I even tell my wife, "This time it's on. I'm doing it, baby." She rolls her eyes and laughs. I'm always surprised at her response. What does she know? I'll show her. Wait until I come home looking like Dwayne "The Rock" Johnson. Roll your eyes then, woman.

Fast Forward

Six months goes by quickly. I haven't seen my gym membership card in four months. It might be under the Whopper wrappers discarded on my nightstand. Or it could have gone through the wash. Who knows?

I look at all the unopened bottles of vitamins on my dresser and wonder if I can return them. My wife is not going to meet Dwayne "The Rock" Johnson. She'll have to settle for Robert "The Gut" Cook, but she already knew that.

What's Wrong with me?

I did a Google search and found a disease with all my symptoms. Narcotizing Dysfunction. Was I going to die? Would it be painful? How long did I have?

I read on and was relieved to find it was not fatal. Narcotizing

Dysfunction (I've nicknamed it ND13), is a Sociological condition. Those who suffer from it confuse knowledge with action. The idea is, the more they become informed, the less active they become. They mistake knowing about something and even talking about it as doing something.

They can rationalize not doing anything because they have talked about it and are informed about it.

Wow, that's crazy, but awesome. At least now I could tell my wife I had a legitimate excuse. I was sick.

Serious Condition

While my gym experience is somewhat humorous, when it comes to our spiritual lives, it's no laughing matter.

I experienced some of these symptoms in my faith journey. And I am not alone.

Many followers of Christ have a roller coaster relationship with Jesus. They are on fire in January when they are making New Year's resolutions, and then in February, a cold front rolls in. The fire dwindles to a few embers, and by March, it burns out.

The Vaccine

Unlike the infected Zombies in The Walking Dead, we can be cured from ND13.

I've labeled the vaccine HS1-8. It's found in the Book of Acts chapter one, verse 8:

Jesus said, "But you will receive power when the Holy Spirit comes on you; and you will be my witnesses in Jerusalem, and in all Judea and Samaria, and unto the ends of the earth." (Acts 1:8, NIV)

Inoculation is the placement of a serum or vaccine substance into the body that will grow or reproduce, boosting our immunity to a specific disease. The spiritual vaccine is found in the Holy Spirit. As believers, we have been inoculated with the power of the Holy Spirit.

Get Grafted

The reason we struggle in our walk of faith is because we rely on our own strength to propel us forward in our growth. Self-reliance=failure.

Inoculate means "to graft a scion." (A plant part to be grafted onto another plant.) This is what Jesus was talking about in the parable of the Vine and Branches found in John 15:1-8.

Scripture Minute

The Vine and the Branches

"I am the true vine, and my Father is the gardener. He cuts off every branch in me that bears no fruit, while every branch that does bear fruit he prunes so that it will be even more fruitful. You are already clean because of the word I have spoken to you. Remain in me, and I will remain in you. No branch can bear fruit by itself; it must remain in the vine. Neither can you bear fruit unless you remain in me.

I am the vine; you are the branches. If a man remains in me and I in him, he will bear much fruit; apart from me you can do nothing. If anyone does not remain in me, he is like a branch that is thrown away and withers; such branches are picked up, thrown into the fire and burned.

If you remain in me and my words remain in you, ask whatever you wish, and it will be given you. This is to my Father's glory, that you bear much fruit, showing yourselves to be my disciples."

(John 15:1-8, NIV)

Fight the disease. Get your HS1-8 shot today.
Then tell the rest of the world you found the cure for ND13.

Week 2 Day 5

Don't overdo it

Now that you know I'm not a gym rat let me share with you what I did learn in my sporadic gym attendance.

After not really lifting anything heavier than my PS3 controller for months ... okay, okay, years, I had charged into the gym like Arnold Schwartzinwhatever and piled on the metal plates. I struggled through my workout, and Hulk-like, growled home.

I couldn't walk for three days! My wife had to feed me because I couldn't lift the ridiculously heavy spoon to my mouth. My arms had turned to rubber overnight, and I felt my knuckles drag the ground.

My wife's, "I told you not to overdo it," would have gotten a piece of my mind if I'd had the strength to speak.

Start with the bar

Three months later I dragged myself back to the torture chamber, memories of the pain fresh as open wounds, to ask the personal trainer what he recommended.

He laughed. "I was wondering if you'd be back." Apparently, I put on quite a show the last time I was in, and they were placing bets if I'd ever return.

He suggested I start with the bar. Yes, I had heard correctly. Start with just the bar, no weights. My body was not yet conditioned to deal with a heavy load.

I had to work up to it. Building muscle is a process. I was trying to get buff in one workout. An unrealistic expectation that would cause me to be discouraged, which would actually hinder my progress.

Why hadn't I asked for the trainer's advice three months ago?

Don't set yourself up for failure. You do not have to read the whole

Bible in one month and understand everything. There is a lot to learn from the Bible. I've been reading it for over 20 years, and I make new discoveries all the time. You are not reading to win a race. You are reading to acquire knowledge.

Commit to reading the Bible for five minutes a day to start with. You will enjoy it and look forward to returning to it every day. If you set an unrealistic goal, like reading an hour a day, you are less likely to stick with it.

Caution: Stuff comes up. You'll miss a day, then another. After several weeks, you'll figure why bother, I just don't have the time.

Giving up on reading the Bible is not an option. Just like food is nourishment for the body and necessary for growth, the Word of God is equally necessary for spiritual nourishment and growth.

Scripture Minute

But Jesus told them, "No! The Scriptures say, 'People need more than bread for their life, they must feed on every word of God.'"

(Matthew 4:4, NIV)

Jesus said: It is not the flesh that gives a person life. It is the spirit that gives life. The words I told you are spirit and so they give life.

(John 6:63, NIV)

Your word is a lamp to my feet and a light for my path.

(Psalm 119:105, NIV)

*The unfolding of your words gives light;
it gives understanding to the simple.*

(Psalm 119:130, NIV)

*Direct my footsteps according to your word;
let no sin rule over me.*

(Psalm 119:133, NIV)

Start with the bar

Week 2 Day 6

Facebook through the Bible

If you're like most people, teens, and adults alike, you probably update your Facebook status several times a day. You spend even more time reading your wall and liking your friends' statuses.

While we have countless free time on our hands for these endeavors, we struggle to find any time in our busy day to read the Bible or pray. Between Facebook and Twitter, it's a wonder we even have time to eat.

When I find myself too busy to read my Bible or spend quality time in prayer, I am reminded of a quote: "You make time for what's important to you."

This is true of me. No matter how busy I am, if I really care about something, I get it done. So when we neglect the Word of God because we are too busy on social media, what are we saying about our relationship with God?

Not a guilt trip

I want to propose something to you. Yesterday we talked about starting with the bar, meaning start small. I am going to help you do just that.

Download a Bible app to your phone. Why are you still reading? I mean download it right now, so you don't forget. I'll wait right here.

Okay, great, you're back. I took the opportunity to grab a sandwich.

So this is what I propose: Every time you are going to go onto Facebook or Twitter, stop and go to your Bible app. Read one verse. That's it. Some people are on Facebook so much, they will probably read the whole Bible in a week.

You may even start to find yourself reading more than one verse because the Bible is full of stories about spies, epic battles, crazy kings, betrayal, murder, and even exorcisms. It's like a blockbuster movie.

Scripture Minute

All scripture is God-breathed and is useful for teaching, rebuking, correcting and training in righteousness, so that the man of God may be thoroughly equipped for every good work.

(2 Timothy 3:16-17, NIV)

But seek first his kingdom and his righteousness, and all these things will be given to you as well.

(Matthew 6:33, NIV)

Our priorities reveal what we truly value.

Week 2 Day 7

1) What do you feel is the greatest hindrance to your spiritual growth?

2) What one thing can you do today to overcome this obstacle?

3) On a scale of 1 (dead) to 10 (off the charts awesome), how would you rate your spiritual pulse? Explain.

4) Pick one Bible verse from our devotions this week and memorize it.

5) List some ways that you can find time in your busy day to read and study God's word.

6) List three areas in your life you hope to improve through Bible study.

7) Find someone you trust and respect to hold you accountable to daily Bible reading.

Resistance Training
for Success

Week 3 Day 1

Worm Food

So check this out. This dude Lazarus, Jesus' friend, checks out, as in for good. So they wrap him up in this mummy costume and put him in a tomb. They seal it up with a big stone and go mourn.

Jesus shows up on the scene after Lazarus has been dead for four days, and by now, he's smelling pretty ripe. Everybody's sad and crying. Even Jesus cries.

Jesus goes to the tomb and tells the onlookers to remove the stone from the entrance. They were all like, "Say what? This dude is rotting in there. The stench will be terrible. We won't eat for a week."

Jesus told them to put their belief into action. "Move the stone."

Lazarus Come Forth

Jesus said a little prayer and told Lazarus it was time to get up. The crowd must have thought Jesus had lost his mind, but their eyes were glued to the tomb, just in case. The crowd was amazed when Lazarus, dressed from head to toe in his mummy suit, appeared at the entrance. Jesus ordered them to remove his grave clothes.

Lazarus had been dead but was brought to life by Jesus. He had been entombed in that nasty, stinky grave, rotting in the dark. Now, he was out in the light, and he felt great.

Chillin' In The Crypt

How ridiculous would it have been if Lazarus, after being raised from death to life, after escaping that smelly, dark tomb, how ridiculous would it have been if he occasionally went back in the tomb to hang out? Not all the time, just sometimes.

I know this sounds ludicrous, and we know Lazarus would never do that, but we would, and we do.

What's He Talkin' About?

You know exactly what I'm talking about. It just sounds terrible when we say it out loud. Okay, so maybe you are not hanging out in your local graveyard, but that's just a metaphor for your old sinful life.

Here's the reality, like it or not. Jesus brought us from death to life. We were dead, and He pulled us from the stench of our sin and removed our grave clothes. He clothed us in garments of righteousness.

The old was gone. The new was now. We felt alive for the first time in our lives. We loved God with everything in us. We ran from evil and clung to Christ. We shared our joy with everyone. We read our Bibles and enjoyed it. We prayed to God without asking for stuff. We loved our new life.

But

Excitement dwindles and becomes complacency. Love becomes obligation. We start to look back ... to the tomb. Our old life. After being brought from death to life, after experiencing the power of Jesus in our life, after the sacrifice He made on the cross for us, we go back into the tomb. Into the stench, into the darkness. Into the bondage of the grave clothes. We turn from our new life in Christ and return to our old ways.

Jesus replied, "No one who puts a hand to the plow and looks back is fit for service in the Kingdom of God." (Luke 9:62, NIV)

Don't Look Back

I'm not referring to the hit song from the band Boston. You can't start the next chapter of your life if you keep rereading the last one.

The Apostle Paul gave us some great advice: *"...But one thing I do: forgetting what lies behind and straining forward to what lies ahead, I press on toward the goal for the prize of the upward call of God in Christ Jesus."* (Philippians 3:13,14, ESV)

Scripture Minute

Forget the former things; do not dwell on the past.
See, I am doing a new thing! Now it springs up; do you not perceive
it?
I am making a way in the desert and streams in the wasteland.

(Isaiah 43:18-19, NIV)

Therefore, if anyone is in Christ, he is new creation. The old has
passed away; behold, the new has come.

(2 Corinthians 5:17, ESV)

Stay out of the tomb, it stinks.

Week 3 Day 2

Caution, Falling Rocks

When I was little, I always wondered how the rocks could read and know just where they were supposed to fall. As I got older and a bit wiser, I learned that the powers-that-be simply placed these signs where the conditions provided the highest probability of a rock slide.

It also explained why they put deer crossing signs on busy highways. I always thought they should let the deer cross on rural back country roads that were less traveled. Seemed safer for everyone involved.

Warning: Danger Ahead

Whenever I see a sign that says "High Accident Area," I quickly pull over and whip out my cell phone in hopes of making a viral video. On a serious note, I focus my attention on my surroundings. I look for possible situations, so I'm not taken by surprise.

These signs, when heeded, prevent tragedies. Bridge freezes before road, sharp curve ahead, caution, hidden driveway.

Someone either saw a potentially dangerous situation or something bad already happened at these locations. In an effort of prevention, warning signs were installed.

Give me a break Dad

My kids think I'm paranoid because I am always yelling as they run out the door; "Wear a helmet, look both ways, wear your seat belt!"

To them, I am just hindering their good time. In reality, I don't want them to crack open their head, get hit by a car, or hurt in an accident.

When I first started reading the Bible and saw all the warnings listing all the things I should not do, I looked at it as God crushing on my fun.

In reality, God sets boundaries to protect you and me from self-destructive behavior or from people out to harm us.

One-night stand

Think about the commandment not to commit adultery. Adultery destroys marriages, tears families apart, ruins kids, and occasionally ends in murder.

So while trying to escape an unhappy marriage by sneaking off to a secret rendezvous at a cheap motel seems exciting in the moment, God sees the end result long before you do.

Remember

Satan hates you and wants to destroy you.

God loves you and wants to protect you.

Scripture Minute

If you fully obey the LORD your God and carefully follow all his commands I give you today, the LORD your God will set you high above all the nations on earth. All these blessings will come on you and accompany you if you obey the LORD your God.

(Deuteronomy 28:1-2, NIV)

And you must always obey the Lord's commands and decrees that I am giving you today for your own good.

(Deuteronomy 10:13, NLT)

Be alert and of sober mind. Your enemy the devil prowls around like a roaring lion looking for someone to devour.

(1 Peter 5:8, TNIV)

Which voice will you listen to?

Week 3 Day 3

Snowed In

One snowflake will not send the masses scrambling to the store to buy large quantities of milk, bread, and eggs, or cause alarm and close the schools. One snowflake will most likely go unnoticed.

But what happens when that snowflake bands together with a few billion more? They become a force to be reckoned with. They can shut a city down, bring major transportation to a standstill and put smiles on the faces of many children.

One snowflake can be ignored. Millions cannot. One snowflake, united with other like-minded snowflakes bent on covering the landscape, can transform a barren wasteland into a beautiful winter wonderland in a relatively short period of time. One snowflake bears no weight. Millions of snowflakes can collapse roofs and snap tree branches.

So what's my point?

Like a single snowflake, your effect in your community might be minimal. Your voice for truth can be drowned out in a chorus of lies.

But when you come together with a group that is united and determined to make a difference in their community, you will not be so easily dismissed.

People take notice

If you rode your bike through town on a Saturday afternoon, you might not even be noticed. You would blend into your everyday surroundings.

But if several hundred of your friends formed a flash mob and rode hundreds of bikes through your town, you would cause quite a stir. People would break out their cell phones and take video. People would wonder what was going on. What are you up to? They could not ignore you.

What if each one of you had the same shirt on, featuring a specific website. How many people do you think would immediately look up that site? How many of those people would go on to tell their friends and family about what they witnessed that day? How many of the same people would post their video to Facebook and YouTube?

This is why it is important to come together as the Church. The Body of Christ. Without the church, you stand alone, like the single snowflake that quickly melts. The solitary Christ follower tends to melt under temptation and turn from God quickly.

2 R Better Than 1

That was King Solomon's tweet on things. Let's check on Ecclesiastes 4:9-12 (NIV):

"Two are better than one, because they have a good return for their work: If one falls down, his friend can help him up. But pity the man who falls and has no one to help him up! Also, if two lie down together, they will keep warm. But how how can one keep warm alone? Though one may be overpowered, two can defend themselves. A cord of three strands is not quickly broken".

When your community encounters a group of sold-out followers of Christ, determined to impact the people in their community for the cause of Christ, they will not be able to ignore you. Your actions will be noticed and the results undeniable.

Like the bike riders in my story wearing the same shirts and sporting their church's website. Your group clothed together bringing Christ's message of love comes with enough power to bring down Satan's strongholds in people's lives.

Scripture Minute

Let us not give up meeting together, as some are in the habit of doing, but let us encourage one another- and all the more as you see the Day approaching.

(Hebrews 10:25, NIV)

For where two or three come together in my name, there am I with them.

(Matthew 18:20, NIV)

They devoted themselves to the apostles' teaching and to the fellowship, to the breaking of bread and to prayer.

(Acts 2:42, NIV)

So Christ himself gave the apostles, the prophets, the evangelists, the pastors and teachers, to equip his people for works of service, so that the body of Christ may be built up...

(Ephesians 4:11-12, NIV)

Don't be a lone wolf
Travel with your pack

Week 3 Day 4

Embrace Trials

You probably read the title of today's devo and thought, *Yeah right. You must not have faced anything hard, like I have!*

I came from an abusive, broken home. I suffered sexual abuse from a close relative before I was 10. After my father left, we suffered extreme poverty. I was bullied at school. I was arrested for the first time at 11 years old. I know the pain of infidelity. I suffered when my ex-wife absconded with our children, and I didn't see them for over 18 years. And just a short time ago, my younger brother, whom I loved with all my heart, hung himself. My nineteen-year-old son, also hung himself.

I know what it is to face trials of many kinds.

That's why I can say with complete assurance, those trials prepared me for the calling God placed on my life. Just like Joseph, for such a time as this. These trials were not easy but necessary.

James Must Be Crazy

James tells us to consider it pure **JOY,** whenever we face trials of many kinds. Say what? Joy? Really? And notice he did not say, **IF** you face trials, but whenever, as in—it will be more than once.

So let me get this straight. Not only am I going to face trials, but I should be joyful when I do?

Why?

Because these trials have a purpose. According to James, they develop perseverance (which means doing something despite difficulty or delay in achieving success). And perseverance **MUST** finish its work (in us), so that we can be mature and complete, lacking nothing.

Did you catch that? These trials are necessary. Yes, the very trials that cause us to question God's sovereignty or calling in our life. The trials that cause doubt to creep in. The situations that would have us believe God is asleep at the wheel, are actually allowed by God for our benefit, to bring about his will in our life.

Sounds messed up I know

But James tells us to embrace these trials because they are vital to our growth. He goes so far as to say, without these trials, we will not grow up. If you take nothing else from this, catch this: James says the testing of your faith develops perseverance, and perseverance MUST finish its work so that we may be complete.

Without Trials, We Would Be Incomplete

The next time you face trials, Satan would have you believe God is turning His back on you, but remember, God is perfecting you.

Scripture Minute

Consider it pure joy, my brothers, whenever you face trials of many kinds, because you know that the testing of your faith develops perseverance. Perseverance must finish its work so that you may be mature and complete, not lacking anything.

(James 1:2-4, NIV)

"I have told you these things, so that in me you may have peace. In this world you will have trouble. But take heart! I have overcome the world."

(John 16:33, NIV)

We are hard pressed on every side, but not crushed; perplexed, but not in despair; persecuted, but not abandoned; struck down, but not destroyed. We always carry around in our body the death of Jesus, so that the life of Jesus may also be revealed in our body.

(2 Corinthians 4:8-10, NIV)

The Spirit himself testifies with our spirit that we are God's children. Now if we are children, then we are heirs-heirs of God and co-heirs with Christ, if indeed we share in his sufferings in order that we may also share in his glory. I consider that our present sufferings are not worth comparing with the glory that will be revealed in us.

(Romans 8:16-18, NIV)

No pain, no gain

Week 3 Day 5

Expect the Worst

If you were walking alone in a seedy back alley at midnight, your 'spidey' senses would be heightened. In fact, you'd expect danger.

If you could visually see the spiritual realm, 2 o'clock on a sunny Sunday afternoon would hold just as much danger as that dark alley.

Satan's minions, masters in the art of deception and destruction, are lurking, setting traps, waiting to snare you. It's their 24/7 job. Your best chance at avoiding these snares they have set for you is knowledge.

If you recognize the trap, you stand a better chance of avoiding it.

If It Looks Too Good ...

it probably is. No matter how good a situation looks, you need to question everything. Does this situation lead me closer to God or will it take me further away? Will this situation, though good, keep me from experiencing great? This is important because good is the enemy of great.

Good is the method Satan employs the most. When you settle for good, you never realize all you have compromised.

For false messiahs and false prophets will appear and perform great signs and wonders to deceive, if possible, even the elect. (Matthew 24:24, NET)

The Art of War

Knowing your enemy is the key to victory.

"Know your enemy and know yourself and you can fight a hundred battles without disaster" (Sun Tzu, The Art of War).

Game Advantage

I love the Call of Duty game franchise, and I stand in line with my boys at every midnight release. The first time I play the game on campaign mode, I make it a few minutes and get killed by unexpected hidden enemies or sudden ambushes. I get to try this level again, but this time, I know what to expect, and I make it a little further. I repeat this until I beat the game. The second time I play the game, I know where the enemy is, and I expect the attacks, so I am prepared. I know what to avoid and when to fight. I beat the game quickly and almost effortlessly.

Now, when one of my sons plays the game, I can coach them and tell them where the danger is. They don't make the same mistakes I made, and they don't suffer as many casualties. This is why sales of Game strategy guides exist and sell so well.

Strategy Guide to Life

Your life experiences and the Bible are your strategy guide to successfully help you navigate the enemy's territory and beat him at his own game.

Scripture Minute (Cheat Codes)

How can a young man keep his way pure?
By living according to your word.

(Psalm 119:9, NIV)

Whether you turn to the right or to the left, your ears will hear a
voice behind you saying, "This is the way; walk in it."

(Isaiah 30:21, NIV)

Do not let this Book of the Law depart from your mouth; meditate
on it day and night, so that you may be careful to do everything
written in it. Then you will be prosperous and successful. (spiritually)

(Joshua 1:8, NIV)

All Scripture is God-breathed and is useful for teaching, rebuking,
correcting and training in righteousness, so that the man of God may
be thoroughly equipped for every good work.

(2 Timothy 3:16-17, NIV)

Download your cheat codes into your memory today
Defeat the enemy and win the game

Week 3 Day 6

Schoolyard Bully

This week, I hope you figured out that Satan is the bully that pops out of the bushes with his minions and steals your lunch money. He's the wedgie-giving kid that punches you in the back of the head on the bus, trips you in the hallway, steals your homework and stuffs you in your locker.

Just like every other bully, Satan tries to get inside your head and project himself as bigger and badder than he really is. He feeds on your fear and wants you to feel helpless to fight against him.

Here's the good news ... literally

Paul assures us we have already won when we put our trust in Jesus. Let's check out a couple verses on the subject:

You, dear children, are from God and have overcome them, because the one who is in you is greater than the one who is in the world. (1 John 4:4, NIV)

For God has not given us a spirit of fear and timidity, but of power, love, and self-discipline (2 Timothy 1:7, NLT).

As it is written: "For your sake we face death all day long, we are considered as sheep to be slaughtered." No in all these things we are more than conquerors through him who loved us (Romans 8:26-27, NIV).

Take a stand

When you stand up to a bully, he generally backs down. If you stood up to the bully with the principal standing next to you, the bully would definitely back down.

So get this

God is always with you, and Satan is afraid of God. He has already been defeated. He just puts on a big act for you, but once you realize the truth, he no longer has any power over your life. Realize, the only power Satan ever really had over you, was the power you gave him.

Scripture Minute

Submit yourselves therefore to God.
Resist the devil, and he will flee from you.

(James 4:7, ESV)

Put on the whole armor of God, that you may be able to stand
against the schemes of the devil.

(Ephesians 6:11 ESV)

No temptation has overtaken you that is not common to man. God is
faithful, and he will not let you be tempted beyond your ability, but
with the temptation he will also provide the way of escape, that you
may be able to endure it.

(1 Corinthians 10:13 ESV)

Resist the devil
Send him packing

Week 3 Day 7

Today, I want to help you develop some resistance techniques. Reading scripture is only beneficial if you apply it. Just knowing it is not enough. Application causes growth, and growth leads to the transformation of your heart and mind.

As your mind and heart is transformed into the mind and heart of Christ, you will be able to stand against Satan and his schemes. When you resist, he will flee from you.

1. *"No temptation has seized you except what is common to man. And God is faithful; he will not let you be tempted beyond what you can bear. But when you are tempted, he will also provide a way out so that you can stand up under it."* (1 Corinthians 10:13, NIV)

2. Paul is not saying you won't be tempted, but that when you are, God will provide a way for you to resist. But God does not do the work for us. We still have a choice. Do we take the way out, or do we embrace the temptation and act on it?

Put an evacuation plan in place before the storm of temptation comes. Where do you escape to? A friend or accountability partner? Where do you go? Youth group or church? Maybe an NA or AA meeting? Develop the plan before you need it.

3. *My son, if sinners entice you, do not give into them* (Proverb 1:10, NIV).

"When tempted, no one should say, 'God is tempting me.' For God cannot be tempted by evil, nor does he tempt anyone; but each one is tempted when, by his own evil desire, he is dragged away and enticed. Then after desire is conceived, it gives birth to sin; and sin, when it is full-grown, gives birth to death." (James 1:13-15, NIV)

4. Here's some simple advice, STAY OUT of the seedy alley. Avoid situations where you may be tempted. Don't go to the party where everyone will be drinking. Don't get into an intimate situation with a boyfriend or girlfriend where it will be hard to resist sexual sin. *And do not give the devil a foothold* (in your life) (Ephesians 4:17, NIV).

5. *"Finally, brothers and sisters, whatever is true, whatever is noble, whatever is right, whatever is pure, whatever is lovely, whatever is admirable--if anything is excellent or praiseworthy--think about such things."* (Philippians 4:8, TNIV)
   "Set your minds on things above, not on earthly things. For you died, and your life is now hidden with Christ in God." (Colossians 3:2,3, NIV)

6. So here it is in plain English: Relationships for Dummies. If you are spending every minute with your girlfriend, it will be real hard to fall for another girl, right? You will not have an opportunity to cheat on her. You would probably not even have the desire.

Same result. If you are spending all your time with God and focusing on his will for your life, you will not have the time or the desire to fall for Satan and his schemes.

7. I leave you with the best advice of all:
   "Submit yourselves, then, to God. Resist the devil, and he will flee from you." (James 4:7, NIV)

Developing New
Healthy Habits

Week 4 Day 1

I'll be back

When Arnold Schwarzenegger spoke these three words in the movie, The Terminator, it meant it was going to get ugly. But as bad as Arnold was, he ain't got nothing on the Devil.

As you empty your life of the bad, you need to fill it quickly with good things, or the bad will come back with a vengeance.

Status update from Jesus

"When an evil spirit comes out of a man, it goes through arid places seeking rest and does not find it. Then it says, 'I will return to the house I left.' When it arrives, it finds the house swept clean and put in order. Then it goes and takes seven other spirits more wicked than itself, and they go in and live there. And the final condition of that man is worse than the first" (Matthew 12:33-35, NIV).

Knock, Knock, Sarah Connor?

Like the cyborg terminator, Satan seeks to kill and destroy without remorse. Once you evict him from your life, do not allow him to rent space in your life again.

Empty Vessels

So you've poured out all the sludge from your vessel and went thru God's powerful dishwasher, so now what? What should you fill your life back up with?

Therefore, if anyone cleanses himself from what is dishonorable, he will be a vessel for honorable use, set apart as holy, useful to the master of the house, ready for every good work (2 Timothy 2:11, ESV).

All you need is love

No, not for some girl you think is hot. Not the kind of love you have for Mt. Dew either. Jesus not only loved but was willing to die for the very people who hated him. Love is a great habit to develop so is being Christ-like. Let's check the Bible for some clarification:

Be imitators of God, therefore as dearly loved children and live a life of love, just as Christ loved us and gave Himself up for us, as a fragrant and sacrifice to God (Ephesians 5:1-2, NIV).

Sacrificial Love

What the heck does it mean to fill our life with sacrificial love? Apparently, a lot to God, like a whole lot. 1 Corinthians 13:3 tells us, if we give away everything we have to the poor and surrender ourselves to be burned at the stake, but have not love, we gain nothing.

We can know all the mysteries of the universe and have faith so strong that we can toss mountains around with the flick of a finger, but without love, we have nothing.

Sounds easy enough right?

Wrong. What? How can it be hard to love people when they are so nice to us?

Okay, you got me on this one, but here's the hard part, so listen up.

How'd this wrench get in here?

"You have heard that it was said, 'Love your neighbor and hate your enemy.' But I tell you: Love your enemies and pray for those who persecute you, that you may be sons of your Father in heaven (Matthew 5:33-34, NIV).

If you love those who love you, what reward will you get? And if you only greet your brothers, what are you doing more than others? Do not even pagans, (unbelievers) do that (Matthew 5:36-37, NIV)?

The Bar Has Been Set

The word Christian means Christ-like. Jesus not only loved the very people who crucified him, but willingly laid down his life for his enemies. So, to be called a Christian is to love our enemies.

Scripture Minute

Whoever claims to live in him must live as Jesus did.

(1 John 2:6, NIV)

Follow my example, as I follow the example of Christ.

(1 Corinthians 11:1, NIV)

Bless those who curse you, pray for those who mistreat you.

(Luke 6:28, NIV)

It's hard to consider a man your enemy
when you are praying for him
Get to praying!

Week 4 Day 2

Tame your tongue

The hardest part for the newer Christian is controlling what they say. I was a professional profanity artist and very creative when it came to inventing new combinations of curse words. I was a contractor, and part of a contractor's resume is the ability to use the f-word proficiently. I mastered the technique at a young age and could hold my own with the best of them.

When I made the decision to surrender my life to Christ, I knew I could no longer use vulgar language and still be a good witness. Back in the day, I would curse without realizing it. Now, every time I hear foul language, it echoes in my spirit.

James drops an F-bomb

Not that kind. Check this out:

"We all stumble in many ways. Anyone who is never at fault in what they say is perfect, able to keep their whole body in check. When we put bits into the mouths of horses to make them obey us, we can turn the whole animal. Or take ships as an example. Although they are so large and are driven by strong winds, they are steered by a very small rudder wherever the pilot wants to go.

Likewise, the tongue is a small part of the body, but it makes great boasts. Consider what a great forest is set on," (F-bomb coming), *"FIRE by a small spark. The tongue also is a FIRE, a world of evil among the parts of the body. It corrupts the whole body, sets the whole course of one's life on fire, and is itself set on fire by hell."* (James 3:2-6, NIV)

Polly want a cracker?

The tongue is a troublemaker. James says it's easier to train a whale to ride a unicycle, or maybe it was a parrot to talk than it is to tame our tongue.

Let's check it out.

All kinds of animals, birds, reptiles, and sea creatures are being tamed, and have been tamed by mankind, but no human being can tame the tongue. It is a restless evil, full of deadly poison (James 3:7-8, NIV).

I wish James would not sugar coat things. LOL. So yeah, wow! Our tongue is a restless evil, boastful, arsonist, full of deadly poison. Not something your Grammy would needlepoint on a pillow.

Silver-tongued Devil

James goes on to warn us about talking out of both sides of our mouth. He says we praise God and curse the very humans God created in his likeness. We use our mouth to praise and curse. How whacked is that? Not a very good testimony, huh?

James challenges us with some eye-opening questions:

Can both freshwater and saltwater flow from the same spring? My brothers, can a fig tree bear olives, or a grapevine bear figs? Neither can a salt spring produce fresh water? (James 3: 11-12, NIV).

Impossible? Not with God

So James starts out telling us that no man can tame the tongue, but then he tells us that we should not have an untamed tongue. What gives?

Here's the trick, if we can even call it that. James said no human could tame the tongue, but that leaves the door wide open for the only one who can ... God.

We can overcome our inability by allowing God to transform our hearts and minds and yes, even our tongues. Ask God to change you. Ask God to keep your words pure.

Scripture Minute

Whoever would love life and see good days must keep his tongue from evil and his lips from deceitful speech.

(1 Peter 3:10, NIV)

Do not let any unwholesome talk come out of your mouths, but only what is helpful for building others up according to their needs, that it may benefit those who listen.

(Ephesians 4:29, NIV)

It's not what goes into your mouth that defiles you; you are defiled by the words that come out of your mouth.

(Matthew 15:11, NLT)

Let your conversation be always full of grace, seasoned with salt, so that you may know how to answer everyone.

(Colossians 4:6, NIV)

Nor should there be obscenity, foolish talk or coarse joking, which are out of place, but rather thanksgiving.

(Ephesians 5:4, NIV)

Those who consider themselves religious and yet do not keep a tight rein on their tongues deceive themselves, and their religion is worthless.

(James 1:26, TNIV)

Talk the walk

Week 4 Day 3

You're an idiot

Those three little words probably took you off guard, but you realize this is just a book, and I'm not really calling you an idiot personally.

But how do you feel in school or at home when someone says things to you that are mean and ugly? When I was little, I had a rhyme I would recite when kids called me names. It went like this: 'Sticks and stones may break my bones, but names will never hurt me.'

In reality, that was a lie. I'd rather get hit with a big stick because a physical wound heals, but emotional wounds can last a lifetime. Words are stronger than any UFC star or bodybuilder could ever hope to be. They have the power to encourage a child to grow up and be president or to take their own life at 13.

Self-esteem is very fragile and can be shattered with a few careless words.

When we shatter someone's self-esteem and character, we can apologize, but the damage is done. The person is hurt.

Great Advice

As always, the Bible has the perfect solution for this situation. That's why I just laugh when people say, 'The Bible was written thousands of years ago, how can it be relevant today?'

Easy. Because truth is timeless. So let's check out that relevant book.

Do not let any unwholesome talk come out of your mouths, but only what is helpful for building others up according to their needs, that it may benefit those who listen (Ephesians 4:19 NIV).

Golden Rule

If you get in the habit of treating people the way you want to be treated, you will not have to worry about hurting someone's feelings or crushing their spirit.

Jesus, as always, gave a simple command regarding this:

Do to others as you would have them do to you (Luke 6:21, NIV).

In other words, if you don't want someone doing or saying something to you, don't do it to them. If you live by this code, life is a whole lot smoother.

Scripture Minute

Be kind and compassionate to one another, forgiving each other, just as in Christ God forgave you.

(Ephesians 4:32, NIV)

My command is this: Love each other as I have loved you.

(John 15:12, NIV)

Do not gloat when your enemy falls;
when he stumbles, do not let your heart rejoice,

(Proverbs 24:17, NIV)

Be devoted to one another in love. Honor one another above yourselves.

(Romans 12:10, TNIV)

If it is possible, as far as it depends on you, live at peace with everyone.

(Romans 12:18, NIV)

Don't mix bad words with your bad mood
You will have plenty of opportunities to change a mood,
but you'll never get the opportunity to replace the words you spoke

Week 4 Day 4

I Love My Truck

I just got my truck back after getting a new transmission installed. I immediately took it to a local garage to get it inspected and all legal. It passed for less than $300.00. I had not driven my truck in a year and a half. I washed and waxed it until the black paint had a mirror finish then detailed my 20-inch chrome rims.

I vacuumed the interior, purchased new Zombie Response Team logo seat covers and secured my zombie bobble head strategically on the dashboard so I could see his head rockin' to the beat. My truck looked sick, as in awesome.

I love my truck because it was a gift from my close friend, Art Robin. Art died unexpectedly from a brain aneurysm just months after giving me this gift.

This may sound crazy to some, but I feel better about everything when I am driving it, cruising down the highway.

Forgotten Treasure

Years ago, I rented a house that had a garage. When I opened the garage door for the first time, I found a metallic red 1979 Triumph Spitfire convertible. It was gorgeous. There were no scratches or dents on the body, and the tan leather interior was immaculate. The top of the car door came to my knees. It was love at first sight.

I called my landlord to inquire about the car. He had forgotten the car was in the garage where he had stored it for years. I asked if he wanted to sell it, and he had a better idea.

He asked if I would be willing to paint the interior of the house in exchange for the car.

Say What?

I must be dreaming. This guy wants to give me this beautiful red convertible sports car for painting the house I was living in? So let me get this straight. I'm going to make the house I live in look awesome with a new paint job, and I'm getting a sports car?

Hmmmm … let me think about this. Before I could blink, I said deal.

Rolling, Rolling, Rolling

The landlord let me pick the colors, and I rolled all the walls and ceilings in the house. Three weeks' worth of labor, and I had a new classic red convertible sports car.

In between painting, I spent quite a bit of time sitting in the car pretending to be cruising. I could not start it up because the landlord would not give me the keys until the house was done.

Mine, Mine, All Mine

Finally, the big day arrived. I had finished painting the house, and the landlord and I took care of the obligatory details at the auto tag office, and I was handed the keys. I raced home and ran to the garage, screwed my new license plate on and jumped in the driver's seat without opening the door. I put the key in the ignition and waited for the roar of the engine.

Silence

The engine did not turn over, or even try. I tried 20 more times with the same results. My elation turned to frustration. I quickly called my landlord. "The battery is probably dead. The car has been sitting for 20 years." His voice implied my stupidity. I quickly bought a new battery and installed it.

Ta-da

I turned the key … I turned the key … I turned the key … I tur …

All Show No Go

To make a long, depressing story short and depressing, I never got the car running. The motor was seized and would need to be replaced. The car was built in Britain or England or Timbuctoo, for all I know. It would cost thousands of dollars. Thousands I did not have. Whether or not my landlord knew this, I don't know. I assume since he did not even remember the car was in the garage, he probably didn't remember it had a blown motor.

Is Your Motor Blown?

I had not thought about that car for over 15 years, but I was reading my Bible, and it suddenly seemed relevant.

By all outward appearances, the little convertible was perfect but what good was it if it was internally non-functioning?

It was useless.

Many professing "Christians" I know go to great lengths to look good on the outside, especially on Sunday mornings, but they are internally non-functioning.

Their prayer life is non-existent, and they don't read the Bible. They don't love others. They hold grudges, gossip, and think only of themselves and the pursuit of their happiness. They look like disciples, but they are in reality, deceivers.

The Master Mechanic

Jesus can look right through the fresh paint and shiny rims and see the blown motor. But his ability goes beyond x-ray vision. He can remove the old engine and install a brand new high-performance engine.

Jesus confronted some blown motors in the Bible, check this out.

"Woe to you, teachers of the law and Pharisees, you hypocrites! You are like whitewashed tombs, which look beautiful on the outside but on the inside are full of the bones of the dead and everything unclean" (Matthew 13:17, TNIV).

New Power Plant Under the Hood

One of those bag of bones guys named Nicodemus realized something was wrong in his heart and came to Jesus for fixing. (John 3:1-21)

Jesus cut straight to the core of the problem: **You must be born again.** No, not just saying some prayer. You need a new heart, new mind, and a new purpose. A complete overhaul.

That's what Jesus does in your life when you give him everything and hold nothing back.

Scripture Minute

Blessed are the pure in heart, for they will see God.

(Matthew 5:8, NIV)

Create in me a clean heart, O God, and renew a steadfast spirit within me.

(Psalm 51:10, NIV)

Above all else, guard your heart, for everything you do flows from it.

(Proverbs 4:23, TNIV)

Come near to God and he will come near to you. Wash your hands, you sinners, and purify your hearts, you double-minded.

(James 4:8, NIV)

For the word of God is alive and active. Sharper than any double-edged sword, it penetrates even to dividing soul and spirit, joints and marrow; it judges the thoughts and attitudes of the heart.

(Hebrew 4:12, TNIV)

It's not about looks, it's about power

Week 4 Day 5

Surrounded by Turkeys

I'm sure you've heard the phrase, "It's hard to soar like an eagle when you are surrounded by turkeys."

You probably knew exactly what that meant. For those of you who don't, you might be a turkey.

On A Serious Note

Here's what's up. When I was young and cool, I used to hang out with, how should I say this delicately? Idiots. To be perfectly honest, I had chosen to hang out with idiots. So what did that make me?

They probably thought I was one of them, and they lovingly accepted me into their clan. If I want to continue the honesty here, I was an idiot, but not just any idiot, no, no. According to my family, I was a **Complete Idiot,** and I wore that title like a badge of honor.

Stupid Is Stupid Does

I was always told if I was going to do something I may as well do it right. With this goal in mind, I mastered the art of stupidity. You could say I majored in it.

I skipped school on a regular basis. I acquired possessions that originally belonged to someone else—okay, okay, I stole things. Lots of things. Like a whole lot of things. I got arrested multiple times.

I faced the possibility of being sent to a juvenile detention center, but as they say . . .

You Can't Fix Stupid

Even faced with the juvenile equivalent of jail, my bad habits were undeterred. I would be placed on probation, told to stay out of trouble, and clean up my act.

The judge cautioned me to find a new group of friends to hang out with because my current friends were leading me down a path of misery. I did not heed this wise man's advice, and I had the opportunity to sit in his courtroom many times.

Deleted

I know what you are thinking, *I don't have to give up my friends. I'm not weak. They can't make me do anything I don't want to.* You are right. They can't make you do anything you don't want to. The problem is eventually you will want to. It's our sinful human nature.

I eventually had to face this reality, and if you have not yet, trust me. You will. You cannot have a close, personal, friendly relationship with drug addicts and thieves and drunks, AKA, your old school friends, and walk this new walk.

You will have to clean out your friends list. I'm not saying you stop caring about them, but you cannot flirt with darkness and remain in the light.

As you grow in your faith and your old friends see a change in you, a change for the better, they will be curious and probably envious of you.

They will see all the good things in your life and how you handle storms when they arise. They may even decide to turn from the dark side and become a Jedi. Well, you know what I mean.

Scripture Minute

Do not be misled: "Bad company corrupts good character." Come back to your senses as you ought, and stop sinning; for there are some who are ignorant of God--I say this to your shame.

(1 Corinthians 15:33-34, NIV)

Walk with the wise and become wise, for a companion of fools suffers harm.

(Proverbs 13:20, TNIV)

Stay away from fools, for you won't find knowledge on their lips.

(Proverbs 14:7, NLT)

Do not make friends with the hot-tempered, do not associate with those easily angered, or you may learn their ways and get yourself ensnared.

(Proverbs 22:24-25, TNIV)

I do not sit with the deceitful, nor do I associate with hypocrites. I abhor the assembly of evildoers and refuse to sit with the wicked.

(Psalm 26:4-5, TNIV)

Do not set foot on the path of the wicked or walk in the way of evildoers.
Avoid it, do not travel on it; turn from it and go your way.

(Proverbs 4:14-15, TNIV)

"Letting go means to come to the realization that some people are a part of your history, but not a part of your destiny."
— Steve Maraboli

Week 4 Day 6

Near Miss

I almost hit a bird on my way to work this morning. The bird flew right in front of my car, three inches above the road.

The first thought that popped into my mind was if I could fly, I certainly would not fly down where the danger is. I would soar high in the sky, above all the danger where nothing could touch me.

Then Why Don't You?

God, in His infinite wisdom, immediately gave me a message, the way he does on an almost daily basis. The thought he cleverly planted in my mind was this.

We Christians, like that bird, fly low and close to danger, AKA sin, every day. God has saved us, and we could soar high as on wings like eagles, but we, like that bird, tend to glide just above the danger of temptation and dip our toes in it.

...but those who hope in the Lord will renew their strength. They will soar on wings like eagles; they will run and not grow weary, they will walk and not be faint (Isaiah 30:21, NIV).

Why?

I had to ask myself, what causes us to go back to the bad stuff after experiencing the greatness of God?

We Forget

Like when we get into a new relationship with someone. We spend every day with them, and they are all we think about. We cannot remember what life was like before we met them.

But then we miss a day to go do something else. One day turns into several, and then a few weeks go by and the relationship suffers and dies.

New Everyday

The best way to keep a relationship from going south is to work at it every day. The same is true of your walk with Christ. Every day you must put effort into your relationship with Jesus. Through prayer and praise. By living out your faith daily.

The great thing is, you don't have to worry about Jesus getting more interested in something else. He never leaves you or forsakes. If your relationship seems rocky, you're the one rocking the boat. If God seems far away from you, you're the one moving away.

A Promise You Can Count On

Keep your life free from the love of money, and be content with what you have, for he has said, "I will never leave you nor forsake you." So we can confidently say, "The Lord is my helper; I will not fear; what can man do to me? (Hebrews 13:5-6, ESV)

It's the Devil's job to get you to fail, to sin, to try to drive a wedge between you and God. He wants you to slip up so he can shame you and make you feel guilty. He knows when you feel guilty, you tend to avoid praying or reading your Bible. If he can do that, his job is easy.

Scripture Minute

"Whoever has my commands and keeps them is the one who loves me. Anyone who loves me will be loved by my Father, and I too will love them and show myself to them.

(John 14:21, TNIV)

Then he said to them all: "Whoever wants to be my disciple must deny themselves and take up their cross daily and follow me."

(Luke 9:23, TNIV)

Seek the Lord while he may be found; call on him while he is near.

(Isaiah 55:6, NIV)

The Lord is near to all who call on him, to all who call on him in truth.

(Psalm 145:18, NIV)

Don't make the devil's job easy.
Make him want to quit.

Week 4 Day 7

1) What are some things you could/need to empty out of your life to make room for God to put things in?

2) What one thing could you eliminate today that would give you more time to dig into the Word of God a little deeper?

3) Our mouth usually gets us in the most trouble. Think before you respond this week and pray before you comment on any social media outlets.

4) Say something good and sincere about every person you come in contact with today. You will be surprised at the results and may continue this practice.

5) Do your thoughts line up with your actions? Does your talk match your walk?
   If not, what are some reasons for the inconsistencies? What can you do to improve in these areas?

6) Who in your life is an anchor holding you back from growing in your faith walk? Distance yourself from them.

7) Who in your life is a catalyst for growth in your faith walk? Move closer to them.

If you do these things, you will start to understand what Christ meant when He said he came that you might have abundant life to the full.

Keep Your Eyes
On the Prize

ILLUMIN8

Week 5 Day 1

Yeah, we lost!

Said no one ever. No one wants to lose. We compete to win. Every football team wants to win the Super Bowl. Every baseball team wants to win the World Series. Hockey players want the Stanley Cup, and every team in the NBA wants to win the championship.

The same can be said for every NASCAR driver, professional golfer, and soccer team. No one trains to lose. Regardless of the sport, the goal is to win.

And, no one joins a team to sit on the bench. They want in the game.

Run the race

The Apostle Paul delivered one of the earliest motivational pep talks 2000 years ago, and it's just as relevant today:

"Do you not know that in a race all the runners run, but only one gets the prize? Run in such a way as to get the prize" (1 Corinthians 9:24, NIV).

Great Advice

Run to win. Sounds too simple. Paul is telling you to get in the game. Get your heart and mind right because attitude sets your altitude. You only go as far as you believe you can.

Walk the Talk

Paul practiced what he preached and lead by example;

"Brothers, I do not consider myself yet to have taken hold of it. But one thing I do: Forgetting what is behind and straining toward what is ahead, I press on toward the goal to win the prize for which God has called me heavenward in Christ Jesus." (Philippians 3:13-14, NIV)

Avoid obstacles

As you strive to walk out your faith, the enemy of your soul will stop at nothing to throw you off course. He wants you to give up, to quit. He wants you to return to your old life.

Paul warned us about the schemes of our adversary, the Devil:

I appeal to you brothers, to watch out for those who cause divisions and create obstacles contrary to the doctrine that you have been taught, avoid them. (Romans 16:17 ESV)

The enemy wants to tear you down. He will use whatever means necessary to accomplish his agenda. He will use family members. He will even use Bible-believing church attendees.

He uses the people closest to you because they can inflict the most emotional harm. When Satan attempts to tear you down, you will find renewed strength in Christ.

And it shall be said, "Build up, build up, prepare the way, remove every obstruction from my people's way." (Isaiah 57:14, ESV).

Scripture Minute

Now I say to you that you are Peter (which means 'rock'),
and upon this rock I will build my church,
and all the powers of hell will not conquer it.

(Matthew 16:18, NLT)

We put no stumbling block in anyone's path,
so that our ministry will not be discredited.

(2 Corinthians 6:3, NIV)

Let us not become weary in doing good, for at the proper time we will
reap a harvest if we do not give up.

(Galatians 6:9, NIV)

"I am sending you out like sheep among wolves. Therefore be as
shrewd as snakes and as innocent as doves."

(Matthew 10:16, NIV)

Rip out the rearview mirror
you're not going back

Week 5 Day 2

Drop and give me 20

Every boxer has a trainer; every team has a coach. Their job is to make sure their fighter or team is ready and able to win. They enforce strict training and exercise regimes, as well as dietary programs. They test for drugs. They study the playbook and scrutinize videos of their games to see where improvement can be made. Their job is to bring out the best in their players.

Get with the program

While it is the coach's job to train and motivate players, it is equally important that the players themselves, are all in. They need to want success for themselves. It's not enough for someone to want good things for me if I do not want them for myself. You hear me?

Some players act the part but secretly they take drugs for enhancement or do not eat properly, and some even get snared in illegal activity. If they don't want success, it will not matter how good the coach is or how bad he wants it for the player.

Up to You

I'm sure as you look at the words, **Personal Trainer**, your first thought is of someone who trains with you one on one, and in most cases, you'd be right. But not here.

You need to be your own personal trainer. Check out what the Apostle Paul has to say on the matter:

The Need for Self-Discipline

Everyone who competes in the games goes into strict training. They do it to get a crown that will not last, but we do it to get a crown that will last forever.

Therefore I do not run like someone running aimlessly; I do not fight like a boxer beating the air. No, I strike a blow to my body and make it my slave so that after I have preached to others, I myself will not be disqualified for the prize.
(1 Corinthians 9:25-27, NIV)

Paul exercises his faith, and his diet consists of the word of God. He pushes himself beyond temptation to achieve success, to win the race.

The Holy Spirit guides him, but he still has a choice, just like those players we talked about. Will he follow the Coach, (Holy Spirit)? Or will he allow himself to be tripped up and disqualified from the prize?

Workout routine

Just doing the minimum will not produce spectacular results. If I want to build up my body, sporadic weightlifting with five-pound dumbbells is not going to do it.

If you want to build up your spiritual strength, you will need to do more than read your Bible for 10 minutes a couple nights a week before you drift off to sleep.

You will need to have a more substantial prayer life than just saying, "Thanks for this food, amen."

Make a plan. Write it down. Work it. Mess Up. Get Up. Never Give up.

It won't be easy. You will have to do things your friends won't do, and you won't be able to do some of the things your friends do. No, it definitely will not be easy, but I can promise you this, it will be worth it.

You made a decision to stand for something while those around you fall for anything. It takes courage and commitment to go against the flow.

Partner Up

Find someone else who wants to make the same commitment as you, and do it together. You can hold each other accountable and lift each other up when you are down.

Life is always better when walking it with someone.

Scripture Minute

As iron sharpens iron, so one person sharpens another.

(Proverbs 27:17, TNIV)

After this the Lord appointed seventy-two others and sent them out two by two ahead of him to every town and place where he was about to go.

(Luke 10:1, NIV)

And let us consider how we may spur one another on toward love and good deeds, not giving up meeting together, as some are in the habit of doing, but encouraging one another and all the more as you see the Day approaching.

(Hebrews 10:24-25, TNIV)

When Moses' hands grew tired, they took a stone and put it under him and he sat on it. Aaron and Hur held his hands up—one on one side, one on the other—so that his hands remained steady till sunset.

(Exodus 17:12, NIV)

Finish strong

Therefore, since we are surrounded by such a great cloud of witnesses, let us throw off everything that hinders and the sin that so easily entangles. And let us run with perseverance the race marked out for us, fixing our eyes on Jesus, the pioneer and perfecter of faith. For the joy set before him he endured the cross, scorning its shame, and sat down at the right hand of the throne of God. Consider him who endured such opposition from sinners, so that you will not grow weary and lose heart.

(Hebrews 12:1-3, TNIV)

All those that have gone ahead of you are cheering you on. You are not alone. They are waiting to say:

**Well done
Great is your reward**

Week 5 Day 3

You hungry?

So check out the book of John, chapter 6, verses 1 to 15, and read the story of how Jesus fed 5,000 hungry dudes plus all their wives and rugrats. I can't even begin to comprehend something so insane, but I want to focus on a part of the story that often gets overlooked.

Yes, it's totally amazing that Jesus took five loaves of bread and two fish and multiplied them into a feast to feed 15,000 plus people, but let's look at a seemingly insignificant character from the story.

The person I am speaking of is the boy with the fish sandwiches. And to answer your question about his insignificance, the Gospel of John is the only book that even records his actions. The story is told in Matthew, Mark, and Luke also, but they do not mention the boy.

Why?

It seems the authors of these books were more focused on the miracle itself and not what made the miracle possible. But I think his actions can open our eyes to what is possible.

Be prepared

Out of 15,000 people, it would seem the boy was the only one prepared. He brought a lunch just in case he needed one. Five loaves of bread and two fish would be quite a lunch for a small boy and might even provide dinner if this Teacher talked into the night.

Give what you have

So here is the young boy clutching his sack lunch, surrounded by 15,000 unprepared hungry people. How many of us would say, "Too bad, you should have planned ahead," or, "It's not my problem." Or even legitimately say, "I only have enough for myself."

The boy took the little he had and gave it to the disciples to in turn give to Jesus. If you think about the scene for a minute, you will understand the significance of his actions.

Picture it, you're just a boy out in the field amongst a throng of people and cannot even see Jesus. All you see is butts. Some men are working their way through the crowd, and you hear that the Teacher needs food. Your stomach has been rumbling, and you were just thinking about breaking out your bread and fish for a nice meal.

Something in you makes you give it to the men instead. They immediately whisk you through the crowd, pushing people aside. Finally, you are standing before the Teacher. They take your lunch and give it to him. Goodbye lunch. You have no way of knowing if it will make its way back to you. You just knew this Teacher, the one you heard amazing stories about, needed your lunch.

The boy willingly surrendered all he had to Jesus, expecting nothing in return.

Jesus performed the miracle, but without the boy and his willingness to give what he had, things would have gone differently. Jesus could have turned rocks into bread, but instead, he chose to do what God likes to do, work through a surrendered life.

Trust Jesus

We are the hands and feet of Jesus. It is important always to remember that. Jesus can do more with a crumb than we can with a whole bread factory. Trust that Jesus will take care of us when we put our life in his hands, whatever that looks like. Jesus' will is better than our will. His plans are better than our plans.

The boy John introduced us to ran his race to win an eternal prize.

Scripture Minute

Those who know your name will trust in you,
for you, Lord, have never forsaken those who seek you.

(Psalm 9:10, NIV)

Do not store up for yourselves treasures on earth, where moths and
rust destroy, and where thieves break in and steal.

(Matthew 6:19, NIV)

And without faith it is impossible to please God,
because anyone who comes to him must believe that he exists and
that he rewards those that earnestly seek him.

(Hebrews 11:6, NIV)

"Here is a boy with five small barley loaves and two small fish, but
how far will they go among so many?"

(John 6:9, NIV)

Hold nothing back from God
He didn't

Week 5 day 4

Add more than you subtract

Every day, you subtract 24 hours from your life. Every day you can add life to your 24 hours. It's your choice.

You can let life happen to you, or you can make life happen.

Live life intentionally

Every day, I intentionally set out to impact someone's life in a positive way. I look for opportunities, and most of the time, I fabricate one.

The Bible's take

Therefore be careful how you walk, not as unwise men but as wise, making the most of your time, because the days are evil. So then do not be foolish, but understand what the will of the Lord is. (Ephesians 5:15-17, NAS)

Paul is telling us to use our time wisely. How does he suggest we do that? By understanding what the will of the Lord is. That is the key, but how do we begin to understand the will of the Lord? Believe it or not, that's actually pretty simple.

Mysterious

Many people believe that God is some distant, mysterious being in the sky that wants their money and is just waiting to zap them for all the bad things they do. Many others believe God expects something from them but won't tell them what it is.

Both of these theories are wrong

God is not distant, He is as close as your heart. How can we know God's will and understand his heart?

The Holy Spirit will reveal God's will and also help you carry it out.

Then you will experience the abundant life Jesus spoke of:

But just as it is written, "Things which eye has not seen and ear has not heard, and which have not entered the heart of man, all that God has prepared for those who love Him." For to us God revealed them through the Spirit; for the Spirit searches all things, even the depths of God. For who among men knows the thoughts of a man except the spirit of the man which is in him? Even so the thoughts of God no one knows except the Spirit of God. (1 Corinthians 2: 9-11, NAS)

The Spirit will reveal God's will and also help you carry it out. Then you will experience the abundant life Jesus spoke of:

The thief comes only to steal and kill and destroy; I have come that they may have life, and have it to the full. (John 10:10, NIV)

I challenge you to positively impact a person's life today. Look for someone to compliment—a cashier, a teacher, or fellow student. Then do it again the next day, and the next, and the …

Scripture Minute

*For it is God who works in you to will and to act
in order to fulfill his good purpose.*

(Philippians 2:13, TNIV)

*Equip you with everything good for doing his will, and may he work
in us what is pleasing to him, through Jesus Christ, to whom be glory
for ever and ever. Amen.*

(Hebrews 13:21, NIV)

*Now it is God who makes both us and you stand firm in Christ.
He anointed us, set his seal of ownership on us, and put his Spirit in
our hearts as a deposit, guaranteeing what is to come.*

(2 Corinthians 1:21-23, NIV)

What will you add to your next 24 hours?

Week 5 Day 5

Hero to Zero

Yesterday, I watched a video titled "Unbelievable Play," thinking I was about to witness an amazing feat on the part of a football player. Though I eventually did see some incredible footage in the second half of the video, the first half made a bigger impact.

Here's the set-up: The quarterback launches the ball, and its intended target makes the catch. He tears up the field, running 78 yards with the opposing team's defense trailing behind. He celebrates as he charges across the goal line for a dramatic touchdown. The ball rolls a few feet and is quickly snatched up by the defense. The guy runs across the entire field and scores a touchdown.

The crowd explodes to their feet. What the heck is going on? He can't do that. The ball was dead, and the offense just scored a touchdown.

Or had they?

Upon review of the tape, it became clear what had happened. The receiver, caught up in the moment, celebrated his impending victory a bit too soon. He had actually dropped the ball at the one-yard line and ran across the goal line empty handed.

Instead of a touchdown, it was considered a fumble. The other team, the enemy so to speak, was right there to take advantage of this young man's mistake.

Don't let your guard down

This young man, caught up in the excitement, took his eye off the objective, which was to get the ball across the goal line. That's it. Period.

He celebrated too soon before the mission was complete. This prevented him from achieving victory. He could not wait to receive the adoration from the fans and hear the thunderous applause. His teammates bombarded him with slaps on the butt and back. While he was soaking up the praise for himself, the enemy snatched the victory from under his nose, and he was oblivious to it.

The young man on the defensive team must have read Ephesians 5:15-16 (NIV):

Be very careful then, how you live—not as unwise but as wise, *making the most of every opportunity, because the days are evil.*

The defensive player certainly made the most of every opportunity. He won the game for his team and became the hero, forever in the annals of YouTube.

What of the ball dropper?

Well this would have been good advice for him to have in mind:

"Be alert and of sober mind. Your enemy the devil prowls around like a roaring lion," (or a defensive lineman), *"looking for someone to destroy."* (1 Peter 5:8, TNIV)

Bottom line

Keep your eye on the mission, don't exalt yourself. Let God do that.

Scripture Minute

For whoever exalts himself will be humbled,
and whoever humbles himself will be exalted.

(Matthew 23:12, NIV)

Be on your guard; stand firm in the faith; be courageous;
be strong.

(1 Corinthians 16:13, NIV)

Humble yourselves before the Lord and he will lift you up.

(James 4:10, NIV)

Humble yourselves, therefore, under God's mighty hand,
that he may lift you up in due time.

(1 Peter 5:6, NIV)

If my people, who are called by my name, will humble themselves
and pray and seek my face and turn from their wicked ways, then I
will hear from heaven, and I will forgive their sin and will heal their
land.

(2 Chronicles 7:14, NIV)

Don't drop the ball!

Week 5 Day 6

All In = All Out

Before you can be sold out on an idea, you have to buy into it. At least if you want to have any passion towards the idea. You can't halfheartedly be passionate about something; it doesn't work. Passion does not allow for any gray areas. It's simply black or white. You have passion or you don't.

If you want to see raw passion in real life, try visiting any small midwestern town during the high school football season.

If you don't care, why should I?

I have met people countless times who have either tried to sell me a product or an idea, and their level of passion usually determined my own level of interest.

If someone pitches a product to me in a dull, monotone dialog, I already know, no matter what they are selling, I ain't buying. You feel me?

On the other hand, I have met people so passionate about a product they were selling, I bought it even if I had no use for it. Their passion was infectious and contagious.

Are you contagious?

Webster defines contagious: spread from one person or organism to another by direct or indirect contact (of an emotion, feeling, or attitude) likely to spread to affect others.

So think about your passion for God and his plans. Are you contagiously passionate?

Do you infect others just by being in the same room with them? Does your passion draw others to Christ?

If the answer is no, it's because you have not gone all in for Jesus. Going all out, affects every area of your life and infects everyone you come into contact with. People will be drawn to you because you offer abundant, overflowing life. Life to the full.

Start Today!

Get in the Word daily and surround yourself with people who are already passionately on fire for God. You will become infected. If you are already on fire for Jesus, go burn someone. Jesus commanded us; *"In the same way, let your light shine before others, that they may see your good deeds and glorify your Father in heaven"* (Matthew 5:16, TNIV). So flip on your high beams.

Further Incentive

Jesus issued a harsh warning with dire consequences for those who were not passionately on fire for God.

I know your deeds, that you are neither cold nor hot. I wish you were either one or the other! So because you are lukewarm- neither hot nor cold- I am about to spit you out of my mouth. (Revelation 3:15,16, NIV)

Basically, Jesus said don't play Christian. You either are or you aren't. When you play, you turn people away. Nobody likes a mouth full of lukewarm water.

Scripture Minute

When Jesus spoke again to the people, he said, "I am the light of the world. Whoever follows me will never walk in darkness, but will have the light of life."

(John 8:12, NIV)

For you were once darkness, but now you are light in the Lord. Live as children of light.

(Ephesians 5:8, NIV)

You are the light of the world. A city on a hill cannot be hidden.

(Matthew 5:14, NIV)

Set the world on fire,
start with your town.

Week 5 Day 7

1) Is there something from your past that is hindering you from running an effective race for Christ? If so, what? Give it to God today.

2) In what ways can you exercise your faith to make it stronger this week? Does your diet consist of a daily dose of the Word of God?

3) Like the young boy who gave up his lunch to Jesus, what seemingly insignificant thing in your life can you surrender and allow Jesus to use in a miraculous way?

4) Are you adding life to your 24 hours? What can you do today to impact someone's life for the kingdom of God?

5) Are you focused on the mission at hand? Do you know and understand God's purpose for your life? The sooner you find out God's purpose for your life, the more complete you will feel.

6) What are you holding onto in your life that is preventing you from going all in with Jesus?

7) This week was about focus and keeping your eyes on the prize. This verse will enable you to keep up your stamina when you find yourself running uphill through struggles and temptation. Memorize 1 Corinthians 2:9 (NIV)

However, as it is written: "No eye has seen, no ear has heard, no mind has conceived what God has prepared for those who love him."

Perseverance Prevails

ILLUMIN8

Week 6 Day 1

Don't buy into Churchianity

No, I did not misspell Christianity. No, I do not need to fire my editor. Yes, I intended to write Churchianity. This week, I want to focus on the difference between Churchianity and Christianity and how perseverance paves the path from one to the other. They may seem the same to the casual observer, but in reality, there is a chasm of difference between the two. One leads to life.

Touchdown

Have you ever seen the YouTube videos where a player scores a touchdown but the fans are not happy? You then realize he was in the wrong end zone. The points don't count. The player thought he was carrying out his objective, but his path did not provide the desired results.

He was confused. The scenery looked the same. They both had goal posts. Both end zones were, well, in the end zone, and the paint on the field looked the same. But our player quickly learned just because something looks like the right thing, does not mean it is. Even though he had the best intentions, his actions proved detrimental to himself and his team.

Don't make the same mistake

Churchianity and Christianity both read the same playbook, so what's the problem? The problem is not the playbook. It's what the player does with the information. To one, it's just a bunch of rules and guidelines that they are obligated to read. To the other, it provides purpose and training for winning the game of life.

Churchianity is concerned with how things look to others. Christianity is concerned with how God looks at things. Churchianity puts church on their schedule. Christianity schedules their life around God. Churchianity gets their fill of the scriptures from a pastor once a week. Christianity can't get enough of God's Word. Churchianity makes church a part of their life. Christianity makes God the center of their life. Churchianity is religion. Christianity is relationship. Churchianity dips its toe in the water. Christianity dives in. Churchianity is about doing the minimum. Christianity kicks it into maximum overdrive. Churchianity gives up in the face of persecution and trouble. Christianity presses in closer to God and presses on.

Scripture Minute
(Wise Words and Powerful Promises)

Let us not become weary in doing good, for at the proper time we will reap a harvest if we do not give up.

(Galatians 6:9, NIV)

Since you have kept my command to endure patiently, I will also keep you from the hour of trial that is going to come upon the whole world to test those who live on the earth.

(Revelation 3:10, NIV)

Blessed is the man who perseveres under trial,
because when he has stood the test, he will receive a crown of life
that God has promised to those who love him.

(James 1:12, NIV)

The road to heaven is paved with perseverance.
Make sure you don't take the dirt road.

Week 6 Day 2

Don't let go

Don't let go, don't let go, just hold on tight. My brilliant advice to my son as he gets dragged through the mud during a game of tug-of-war. But on a serious note, we are going to talk about holding fast to the things of God when we are being tossed about by the storms of life.

Hold on to instruction, do not let it go; guard it well, for it is your life. (Proverb 4:13, NIV)

Moo

Yesterday we covered some differences between Churchianity and Christianity and discovered going to church does not make you a Christian any more than eating a burger makes you a cow. The best way to spot the difference is to see how someone reacts to a bad situation or some turmoil in their life.

When the going gets tough, the Churchian throws in the towel. A Christian rolls up the towel and snaps the enemy with it, square on the butt, and sends him packing. The enemy sends trouble our way in hopes of defeating us and destroying our faith. Churchians fall like dominos in the face of trouble, but Christians cling to the Savior and remember this promise:

Submit yourselves, then, to God. Resist the devil, and he will flee from you. (James 4:7, NIV)

Directionally challenged

Churchianity runs away from God. Christianity runs to God. Satan knows if he can drive a wedge and separate you from God, he wins. He wants to remind you of your sins. He whispers that you are unworthy of God's love. He pokes his finger in your subconscious and stirs up feelings of depression and self-loathing. Churchians throw themselves pity parties, but Christians remind Satan of the cross and his future.

Tell and you're dead meat

When I was a kid, I was bullied. The bully knew that if he could intimidate me and keep me from telling an adult what was going on, he could keep up his relentless assault. He wanted me to believe I had nowhere to turn. He convinced me that if I told someone, it would get worse.

But in reality, he was frightened that I would tell someone because he knew his reign of terror would end. He just hoped I would never realize this truth. For a long time, his plan worked, but eventually, I did tell someone, and he was dealt with. I wished I had told someone much sooner as I would have been spared much pain.

When the enemy attacks, and trust me he will, go right to God. Jesus has got your back. He's the protective big brother. He will step in between you and the devil and send him packing with his pointed tail between his legs.

Don't face your enemy alone. Jesus is ready to jump in.

Scripture Minute

(Because Satan is so relentless in his attacks, I gave you some extra verses. Take a few minutes to let them sink in.)

*But the Lord is faithful, and he will strengthen you
and protect you from the evil one.*

(2 Thessalonians 3:3, NIV)

*My God is my rock, in whom I take refuge, my shield and the horn
of my salvation. He is my stronghold, my refuge and my savior- from
violent people you save me. I called to the LORD, who is worthy of
praise, and have been saved from my enemies.*

(2 Samuel 22:3-4, TNIV)

*So do not fear, for I am with you; do not be dismayed, for
I am your God.
I will strengthen you and help you; I will uphold you
with my righteous right hand.*

(Isaiah 41:10, NIV)

*No weapon forged against you will prevail, and you will refute every
tongue that accuses you. This is the heritage of the servants of the Lord,
and this is their vindication from me.*

(Isaiah 54:17, NIV)

God is our refuge and strength, an ever-present help in trouble.

(Psalm 46:1, NIV)

He who dwells in the shelter of the Most High will rest in the shadow of the Almighty. I will say of the Lord, "He is my refuge and my fortress, my God, in whom I trust." Surely he will save you from the fowler's snare
and from the deadly pestilence.

(Psalm 91:1-3, NIV)

Though I walk in the midst of trouble, you preserve my life. You stretch out your hand against my foes; with your right hand you save me.

(Psalm 138:7, NIV)

The Lord will rescue me from every evil attack and will bring me safely to his heavenly kingdom. To him be glory forever and ever. Amen.

(2 Timothy 4:18, NIV)

The Lord will keep you from all harm- he will watch over your life; the Lord will watch over your coming and going both now and forevermore.

(Psalm 121:7-8, NIV)

Break the chains
The only power Satan has over a Christian is….
None

Week 6 Day 3

Advanced Warfare

While writing this week's devotion on perseverance, I ended up getting to practice what I preach. My son, Christian, had saved up $30.00 towards purchasing a video game, which sells for $59.99 at GameStop.

While we were out shopping, my son wanted to stop at GameStop, which was right next to the grocery store. While we were looking around, we found his game on sale for $39.99. We were pumped because I had enough Power Up Rewards points to get $10.00 off of anything in the store.

We took the last special edition copy of the game to the counter. I gave them my info to look up my number to redeem the coupon, but it did not work. It would not recognize my password or let me change it. I stood at the counter and tried for 25 minutes.

My son told me not to worry about it. He said he would keep saving his money. I was not about to give up. The guy behind the counter told me I might have better luck trying from my laptop instead of my cell phone, so we headed home to try it.

I tried a total of 14 times to reset my password. I failed 14 times. My son again said, "Don't worry about it, Dad." Now I was extremely frustrated at this point, and it sounded so easy to throw in the towel, but what kind of example would I set for my son, right?

So I called customer support and after being on hold for 20 minutes the operator answered, and I told her what we had come up against. She said, "No problem," and proceeded to walk me through the procedure and sent me an email to reset my password so I could print out the coupon. I was feeling good and extremely confident.

It did not work. The operator gave up. She said you have to download Firefox or Google Chrome for it to work, and we parted company. My son, looking dejected, assured me that it was okay, that I had tried everything.

At this point, I wanted to say, "You're right son; I did try, but nothing worked. I'm sorry." But I'm writing about perseverance, and it just seemed wrong to give up. I asked myself, *how could I tell others not to give up, not to quit when things got difficult or seemed impossible if I gave up in the face of difficulty?*

I decided to download Google Chrome and start the whole process over again. Guess what? Yep, it worked. It took almost two hours from the time I started at the store until I had the coupon code.

We went back to the store and got the game for $29.99. Mission accomplished! My son could not stop smiling and thanking me. He kept talking about how I didn't give up, and he could not believe we did it. He literally said it at least 20 times that night, "Thanks, Dad, you are the best." I could not stop smiling either. I was a hero to my son.

Was it frustrating? Extremely. Was giving up easier? Yes. Was persevering difficult? Yes. Was the payoff worth it? You better believe it.

I learned a valuable lesson myself that night, and I'm passing it on to you, so take some notes. When we pray for perseverance, God does not give it to you. *He gives you situations to persevere in.* When we pray for patience, He does not give us patience. He sends us situations in which to practice being patient.

My son and I had a blast that night playing the game. Memories that would not have occurred if I had simply taken the easy way out. Nothing worth it is ever easy. Serving God will not be easy, but the payout is worth it.

Scripture Minute

So I say to you: Ask and it will be given to you; seek and you will find; knock and the door will be opened to you. For everyone who asks receives; those who seek find; and to those who knock, the door will be opened.

(Luke 11:9-10, NIV)

The Parable of the Persistent Widow
Then Jesus told his disciples a parable to show them that they should always pray and not give up. He said: "In a certain town there was a judge who neither feared God nor cared what people thought. And there was a widow in that town who kept coming to him with the plea, 'Grant me justice against my adversary.' "For some time he refused. But finally he said to himself, 'Even though I don't fear God or care what people think, yet because this widow keeps bothering me, I will see that she gets justice, so that she won't eventually come and attack me!'" And the Lord said, "Listen to what the unjust judge says. And will not God bring about justice for his chosen ones, who cry out to him day and night? Will he keep putting them off? I tell you, he will see that they get justice, and quickly. However when the Son of Man comes, will he find faith on earth?"

(Luke 18:1-8 TNIV)

For though the righteous fall seven times, they rise again, but the wicked stumble when calamity strikes.

(Proverbs 24:16 TNIV)

And as for you, brothers and sisters, never tire of doing what is good.

(2 Thessalonians 3:1 TNIV)

Stand firm, and you will win life.

(Luke 21:19 TNIV)

Week 6 Day 4

Rocked

My mother always wanted a garden and spoke of it often. One summer, in my teens, I decided I was going to prepare a spot in our backyard so she could grow some vegetables. I found a shovel in the garage and picked what I thought was the perfect spot and started digging.

Right away, I knew it would not be easy. There were rocks, tons of them, hidden just below the surface. Some were rather large, and the shovel could not penetrate deep enough into the ground to remove any dirt. Within minutes, I was sweating, and my back was burning. I learned quickly. This would not be the perfect spot after all. Jesus spoke of a similar situation in a parable he told, as crowds pressed in on him from all sides. The story was about a farmer planting seeds in four types of soils.

One of those soils was littered with rocks, just like the spot I tried to start my mother's garden in. The farmer threw some seed on the rocky ground and hoped for the best. The seeds sprouted quickly, but their roots could not take hold in the shallow soil and grow due to all the rocks. When the sun came up, the plants were scorched, and they withered.

Clueless

The crowds did not understand how seeds and soils had anything to do with them. Even the disciples were clueless and asked Jesus to explain.

Jesus told them the seed represents the Gospel message and the four soils represent four types of people and the circumstances they find themselves in when they hear the message of Christ and his salvation plan. Jesus said, "The one who received the seed that fell on rocky places is the man who hears the word and at once receives it with joy. But since he has no root, he lasts only a short time. When trouble or persecution comes because of the word, he quickly falls away."

Grow some roots

The only way to reach great heights is to grow to new depths. The deeper you dig into God's Word, the stronger your walk. The deeper you go in your prayer life, the healthier your spirit. A strong walk and healthy spirit enable you to withstand trouble and persecution, and overcome the enemy.

Good soil

Jesus went on to tell of seed that fell on good soil. This seed produced a hundredfold crop. Perseverance makes you good soil, which allows you to produce a great harvest for God's Kingdom.

Dig it

I finally did find the perfect spot and dug my mom a garden that made her very happy. We had fresh vegetables all summer. Good thing I didn't give up.

Scripture Minute

Keep a close watch on how you live and your teaching. Stay true to what is right for the sake of your own salvation and the salvation of those who hear you.

(1 Timothy 4:16, NLT)

I press on toward the goal to win the prize for which God has called me heavenward in Christ Jesus.

(Philippians 3:14, NIV)

Being confident of this, that he who began a good work in you will carry it on to completion until the day of Christ Jesus.

(Philippians 1:6, NIV)

Therefore, my dear brothers and sisters, stand firm. Let nothing move you. Always give yourselves fully to the work of the Lord, because you know that your labor in the Lord is not in vain.

(1 Corinthians 15:58, TNIV)

Winners never quit
Quitters never eat fresh veggies

Week 6 Day 5

It's just not worth it

You are going to have some days, maybe even a week here and there, where you feel like giving up. You tell yourself, *It is just not worth it. Living for God is way too hard.* You're tired of your friends making fun of you. You're sick of the snickering and finger-pointing when you pray over your lunch. You're fed up at being called, *Holy Roller, Bible Thumper,* and *Jesus Freak.*

The real issue

You have two choices concerning these feelings. You can let the thought of giving up fester and grow into a monster that steers you away from God, or you can recognize that the source of these thoughts is planted by the enemy and press on.

Jesus understands, but He does not sugar-coat things. He didn't promise you a trouble-free, easy walk through a rose garden. He promised you the complete opposite. Check this out:

If the world hates you, keep in mind that it hated me first. If you belonged to the world, it would love you as its own. As it is, you do not belong to the world, but I have chosen you out of the world. That is why the world hates you. Remember what I told you: 'No servant is greater than his master.' If they persecuted me, they will persecute you also. If they obeyed my teaching, they will obey yours also. They will treat you this way because of my name, for they do not know the One who sent me. (John 15:18-21, NIV)

Jesus gets it

Right before the soldiers brought Judas to plant his kiss of betrayal, Jesus was in agony because of what he knew was before him. He cried out to God to remove this cup from him, but immediately followed it up with,

"Yet not my will, but yours be done."

Jesus did not want to drink the cup of wrath that was about to be poured out on him for the sins of the whole world, but he knew it was not about him. He knew it was about completing the mission he was called to, and he looked past that moment into eternity.

Jesus knew these trials and persecutions were temporary, and you can take comfort in the same knowledge. Take solace in these words Jesus spoke:

"I have told you these things, so that in me you may have peace. In this world you will have trouble. But take heart! I have overcome the world." (John 16:33, NIV)

Peace out

Jesus revealed the secret to not only overcoming persecution but persevering in the face of it. He said, "so that **IN ME** you may have peace." It's like Jesus bubble wrap. If we are wrapped up in him, even though we are tossed around and beaten down, we will not be permanently broken. We can still have peace—peace in the fact that we are in his hands and peace in the fact that we will spend eternity in his presence.

Scripture Minute

Invincible

But we have this treasure in earthen vessels, so that the surpassing greatness of the power will be of God and not from ourselves; we are afflicted in every way, but not crushed; perplexed, but not despairing; persecuted, but not forsaken; struck down, but not destroyed.

(2 Corinthians 4:7-9, NAS)

Blessed are those who are persecuted because of righteousness, for theirs is the kingdom of heaven.

(Matthew 5:10, NIV)

Rejoice and be glad, because great is your reward in heaven, for in the same way they persecuted the prophets who were before you.

(Matthew 5:12, NIV)

But even if you should suffer for what is right, you are blessed. "Do not fear their threats; do not be frightened."

(1 Peter 3:14, NIV)

Spoiler alert:
We win

Week 6 Day 6

Grounded

If a hot air balloon is stuck on the ground, the view never changes. It will never reach the heights for which it was created, nor will it fulfill its purpose. It was made to soar through the sky and enable its occupants to see things they could never see from the ground.

For a hot air balloon to get airborne, they have to release the weight holding it down. Heavy sandbags make flight impossible. Once the weight is removed, the balloon can accomplish its purpose.

U2

The same is true for you too. If you are bogged down with all the weight of your past, it will be impossible for you to reach new heights or accomplish the purposes for which you were created.

Letting go of your past is the key to persevering in your walk with God. The devil wants you focused on your screw ups and mistakes. He wants you harboring anger and hatred in your heart against those who have wronged you.

Misdirection

The enemy knows if he can keep your mind in the past, you won't focus on the future God has planned for you. Magicians use the technique of misdirection for every trick. Without misdirection, you would see the trick and would not be fooled. Don't be fooled by Satan. Let him know the jig is up, you are on to him and his tricks. Tell him his magic show has been canceled, and he's been run out of town.

The devil has been misdirecting people for thousands of years. Check out how the Apostle Paul dealt with it:

You were running a good race. Who cut in on you and kept you from obeying the truth? That kind of persuasion does not come from the one who calls you. "A little yeast works through the whole batch of dough." I am confident in the Lord that you will take no other view. The one who is throwing you into confusion will pay the penalty, whoever it may be. (Galatians 5:7-10, NIV)

Today is the day to cut those ropes. Release yourself from the burden of carrying all that hurt and pain. Even the stupid mistakes you have made. Jesus has forgiven you. You can't change the past, but you can create a new future. You don't have to stay on the road you are on. Take this exit, there's awesome stuff waiting for you. Besides, you can't write a new chapter if you keep rereading the last one.

Great advice

Paul said, "Do not give the devil a foothold." It reminds me of a sign I saw once in front of a church I've mentioned before and will again because it's true.

> **Don't give the devil an inch, he will become your ruler.**

Leave the past where it belongs. You don't live there, and you ain't going back. Live in the present because that's what it is, a present from God. Set your GPS on God and don't take any detours.

Scripture Minute

...Forgetting what is behind and straining toward what is ahead, I press on toward the goal to win the prize for which God has called me heavenward in Christ Jesus.

(Philippians 3:13-14, NIV)

Forget the former things; do not dwell on the past.
See, I am doing a new thing!
Now it springs up, do you not perceive it?
I'm making a way in the desert and streams in the wasteland.

(Isaiah 43:18,19, NIV)

Therefore, if anyone is in Christ, he is a new creation:
The old has gone, the new has come!

(2 Corinthians 5:17, NIV)

Cut the ropes
3...2...1...
LIFTOFF

Week 6 Day 7

1) We started off this week discussing the differences between Churchianity and Christianity, and how many confuse the two. What position do you lean closer to? Churchian or a Christian? Be honest with yourself and explain.

2) When you face adversity, what are some steps you could take to ensure victory?

3) On day four of this week, we talked about rocky soil and the disadvantages of trying to grow mature plants among the rocks. What type of soil are you? Explain. Think of how you might change this if it is not the right kind of soil.

4) What can you do to effectively grow strong and healthy roots of faith?

5) Think of a time when you faced a difficult situation and did not give up. How did you feel about yourself after overcoming the situation?

6) Can you identify some of the ropes in your life that are binding you to your past?

7) What can you do today to free yourself from them?

8) Have you discovered God's purpose for your life yet? If so, what is it?

9) If not, what steps can you take to reveal His plans for your life?

It's Cardio Week

ILLUMIN8

Week 7 Day 1

Hearty Walk

In week two, we briefly touched on the importance of a healthy heart. But the subject of the heart deserves more than a brief touch, so we will dedicate this week to the condition of your heart.

Paramount to having a healthy body, a healthy heart is also necessary for a healthy spiritual walk. A physically strong heart allows you to be more active and sustain endurance. A spiritually strong heart allows you to persevere through any trial or tribulation.

Healthy Heart = Clean Mouth

I know, it's like saying the ankle bone is connected to the hip bone, but roll with me on this because I'm making a point and a valid one at that. Well, technically, it was a point Jesus made 2000 years ago. Check this out:

A good man brings good things out of the good stored up in his heart, and an evil man brings evil things out of the evil stored up in his heart. For the mouth speaks what the heart is full of. (Luke 6:45, NIV)

Even further back than that, as recorded in the book of Proverbs, written by King Solomon:

Above all else, guard your heart, for everything you do flows from it. (Proverbs 4:23, NIV)

There you have it. The tongue bone is connected to the heart bone, the heart bone is connected to ... well, you get the idea. The heart directly controls the tongue, which opens another can of worms because check out the harsh things James, Jesus' brother, has to say about that little thing in your mouth: *The tongue also is a fire, a world of evil among the parts of the body. It corrupts the whole body, sets the whole course of one's life on fire, and is itself set on fire by hell.* (James 3:6, NIV)

It gets worse. James follows up with this:

But no human being can tame the tongue. It is a restless evil, full of deadly poison. With the tongue we praise our Lord and Father, and with it we curse human beings, who have been made in God's likeness. (James 3:8-9, NIV)

Connect the dots

So I started putting two and two together, 'cause I done gradu8ted, and my brain made a connection. Solomon tells me everything I do flows from my heart. Jesus says my mouth speaks what my heart is full of, and his brother says my tongue is evil and cannot be tamed.

If I speak what's in my heart and my tongue speaks evil and cannot be controlled, could it be that I suffer from a heart condition?

Get your heart right

The heart needs more than a brief touch. Our heart determines everything we do and say. It decides what we do with our time and money. It even decides what we watch and listen to. Get your heart right, and everything else will fall in line.

Scripture Minute

*For where your treasure is, there
your heart will be also.*

(Matthew 6:21, NIV)

*My son, give me your heart and let
your eyes delight in my ways,*

(Proverbs 23:26, NIV)

*Create in me a pure heart, O God, and
renew a steadfast spirit within me.*

(Psalm 51:10, NIV)

**Close your mouth
I can see your heart**

Week 7 Day 2

Misery loves company

I'm sure you know people who are always miserable. They post negative comments on Facebook all the time. They complain about everyone and everything. You want to unfriend them but don't need the drama, so you just unfollow them, so you don't have to deal with their negativity.

Arrrrr!

Their pirate name would be Black Heart because that's where all the garbage flows from. They have a heart condition, and they want others to suffer with them. They sail through life on their ship, the Woe Is Me, and throw pity parties at every port they dock at. It they are not happy, nobody's going to be happy.

The simple cure

King Solomon knew some people like this and wrote a prescription for their illness:

A cheerful heart is good medicine, but a broken spirit saps a person's strength. (Proverbs 17:22, NLT)

Solomon continued:

A peaceful heart leads to a healthy body; jealousy is like cancer in the bones. (Proverbs 14:30, NLT)

Let's face it, life is always going to have its troubles. You can't control every situation, but you can still have peace in the midst of these troubles. If your heart is full of the things of Christ and overflowing through your words and actions and transforming your mind, you will have a cheerful life. You will attract others to the message of the Gospel.

I have found this to be absolutely true. As I write these words this Sunday morning, I write with the knowledge that tomorrow afternoon, we have to put our beloved Boxer, Magic, to sleep. He's a cherished, loved member of our family, and we are deeply saddened. And three days from now on January 7th, it will mark the second anniversary of my brother Rick's suicide. He was just 42.

I cannot control life. (If I could my brother would still be alive and Magic would live forever.) I can, however, control how I respond to terrible situations. I've been able to find peace because I've spent years immersed in God's words and experiencing His promises. That is how I am able to overcome these tragedies.

My attitude is good because my heart is right. My heart is right because it is in the hands of my Savior, Jesus Christ. This knowledge enables me to be cheerful when I have every reason to be miserable. Life will knock you down. You can stay down or get up. It's your decision.

Scripture Minute

And the peace of God, which transcends all understanding,
will guard your hearts and your minds in Christ Jesus.

(Philippians 4:7, NIV)

Peace I leave with you; my peace I give you. I do not give to you as the
world gives. Do not let your hearts be troubled and do not be afraid.

(John 14:27, NIV)

The LORD is close to the brokenhearted
and saves those who are crushed in spirit.

(Psalm 34:18, NIV)

Your heart is fragile
Into whose hands have you entrusted it?

Week 7 Day 3

Matters of the heart

If you win someone's heart, you win the whole person. If you don't win their heart, nothing else matters. Success books state that people buy you before they buy your product, and this is SO true. And not just when we are buying a product or service.

But what does that translate to? What does it look like in the real world?

Let's look at the world of musical reality television shows as a real-world example of this. What makes one talented performer win out over another equally talented performer?

Connection

A connection with your audience is key, and the show's producers take full advantage of this fact. Notice some performers are highlighted with mini vignettes of their background stories. You watch through tears as the young man shares his life story. "My dad left when I was three, and my mom struggled to raise five of us on $100.00 per week, but she died of cancer when I was nine so my grandparents raised me until they were killed in a plane crash. I've wanted to give up, but I need to do this for my mom and my grandparents. They would have wanted this for me. I am also raising all my siblings in a two-room apartment in a bad area. The money this would bring would help us move from our crime-ridden neighborhood and put them through college."

Cue the heart strings

We immediately want this person to win. We are even willing to overlook flaws in their talent. They deserve to win because of all they have been through in life. We vote for them even though Joe Rocker was much better. Why? Because they captured our heart. That is the power of the heart. He who controls the heart controls the mind.

"The heart has its reasons which reason knows not."
—Blaise Pascal

The heart is definitely a mystery but not beyond comprehension. The subject of the heart is mentioned almost 1000 times in the Bible and offers you all the knowledge you need to successfully maneuver through this life, regardless of the situation you are facing.

Why is mastering the heart so important? Because it determines your relationship with God.

Jesus replied, "You shall love the Lord your God with all your heart and with all your soul and with all your might." (Matthew 22:37, NIV)

Jesus started with the heart because He knew everything else would follow. Love begins in the heart. Passion and acceptance grow from love. If you want someone to connect with you, capture their heart. You don't have to have the best product or sales pitch. You don't have to be the most attractive or most talented. You don't have to be the smartest or the funniest.

Wanna know how to capture God's heart? Jesus tells you how:

Blessed are the pure in heart, for they shall see God.
(Matthew 5:8, NIV)

Scripture Minute

Grab your Bible and read
Matthew 5:1-16

Want to move mountains?
Move hearts

Week 7 Day 4

Awkward

Here's something you won't find stenciled on your grandmother's dining room wall or needle pointed on a pillow;

"The human heart is the most deceitful of all things, and desperately wicked. Who really knows how bad it is? (Jeremiah 17:9, NLT)

Or how about this one?

As it is written: "There is no one righteous, not even one; there is no one who understands; there is no one who seeks God. All have turned away, they have together become worthless; there is no one who does good, not even one. Their throats are open graves; their tongues practice deceit. The poison of vipers is on their lips. Their mouths are full of cursing and bitterness. Their feet are swift to shed blood; ruin and misery mark their ways, and the way of peace they do not know. There is no fear of God before their eyes. (Romans 3:10-18, NIV)

These are real Debbie downers and will not draw crowds out to church, so we don't hear the truth, we hear fluff. Fluff packs pews but does not change hearts. Fortunately for you, I'm not a fluffy kind of guy.

This is hard stuff to hear but necessary to bring about the kind of change in your life that results in lives being impacted around you, including your own. Better a truth that heals than a lie that hurts.

Spiritual cardio

A pure heart doesn't just happen to you when you say some "sinner's" prayer. Maintaining a spiritually healthy heart is a daily process. You have to work at it just like you have to work out and eat properly to maintain your physical body and heart. You need to be digging into God's word daily to keep your heart in check. Once you dig spiritual truths from the pages of God's Word, you need to put them into practice. Reading and expecting growth without application is like expecting to sprout muscles because you read a fitness magazine.

Be about it

Don't just talk it, walk it. Put God's Word into practice. When the Bible says, "Love your enemy," love your enemy. When the Bible says, "Give to the poor," give to the poor. When the Bible says, "Honor your parents," you guessed it, honor your parents. See, this ain't rocket science.

Satan would prefer if you didn't read the Bible at all, but if he has to choose, he would prefer you just read it and not live it. Readers of the Word are no threat to his plans. Doers of the Word are nothing but trouble to Satan and his schemes.

Do not merely listen to the word, and so deceive yourselves. Do what it says.

(James 1:22, NIV)

That's how you thwart the enemy. That's how you become pure in heart. That's how you will connect with others. That's how you will have a cheerful life. That's how you will have peace regardless of your circumstances. Folks, that's how it's done. Thank you. Thank you. I'll be here all week.

Scripture Minute

Grab your Bible and read
James 1:19-27

James 2:14-26

Get a pure heart
Kill fluffy

Week 7 Day 5

Is TV bad for your heart?

Say what? You know drugs are bad for your heart. You know eating a diet of fatty food is bad for your heart, but watching TV? Come on. How can that be bad for your heart?

If I were referring to your physical heart, I would say it's not. But I am referring to your spiritual heart, and today, we are going to discuss this issue. We will look at what the Bible says about TV, and in the next couple minutes you may come to the same conclusion.

Although the Bible does not specifically talk about television shows, it specifically discusses every topic that is featured on TV.

Relax, I'm not about to beat you up or take you on a guilt trip for watching certain shows or movies. My intention is just to share this information to make you aware of things you may not have been aware of. Then, once you have the facts, you can decide what to do about it.

Ratings

All movies, television shows, and video games come with a rating to make the viewer or gamer aware of the media content. This enables parents to determine whether they want their children to have access to these games and shows or adults who want to know the content of what they are viewing or playing.

PG: Profanity, violence, brief nudity

PG-13: Strong Profanity, Violence, Nudity, Sensuality, Adult activities or themes, Drug use, Mature themes.

R: Adult themes, Adult Activity, Hard language, intense, persistent violence, sexually-oriented nudity.

I'm sure you will agree, every one of these is present in everything on the market today in varying degrees. Thank you, I knew you would.

Now that we have established this fact, we can look at what the Bible says about these activities.

The Bible's take

Paul gives us some wisdom for living as followers of Christ in his letter to the Ephesians: *But among you there must not be even a HINT of sexual impurity, or of greed, because they are improper for God's holy people. Nor should there be obscenity, foolish talk or coarse joking, which are out of place, but rather thanksgiving. For of this you can be sure: No immoral, impure or greedy person—such a man is an idolater—has any inheritance in the kingdom of Christ and of God.* (Ephesians 5:3-5, NIV)

If we take Paul's words at face value and compare them to the ratings definitions listed above, it should cause us to, at the very least, question the content we take in. Everything Paul warns us to avoid is mentioned in the ratings scale from PG, PG-13, and R ratings.

Paul continues: *For you were once darkness, but now you are children of light (for the fruit of the light consists in all goodness, righteousness and truth) and find out what pleases the Lord. Have NOTHING to do with the fruitless deeds of darkness, but rather expose them. For it is shameful even to mention what the disobedient do it secret.* (Ephesians 5:8-12, NIV)

Clueless

Before I read any of this, I never thought twice about what I was watching. I considered it harmless entertainment, but after reading these passages, I had to reevaluate my thinking. I made the personal decision to change what I put in my heart and mind. I don't shove my decisions on others, but I do share why I don't watch certain things because I know there is a possibility that there are people out there as clueless as I was. Maybe you?

The devil likes to keep us in the dark to the things of God because his job is easier that way. We sin out of ignorance, not malice. When we are armed with the facts and act on them appropriately, the devil's job becomes more difficult, if not impossible.

Scripture Minute

Grab your Bible and read
Ephesians 4:17-32

Today, your eyes are no longer closed.
You decide if they stay opened

Week 7 Day 6

Pumped

The heart is a vital organ, pumping blood throughout the body and keeping our other organs alive. Humans can actually live without a brain. According to women, men have been doing it for centuries, but without a heart, we are doomed.

Okay, bad joke, but on a more serious note, our physical heart health is vital to our existence. And just as equally important is our spiritual heart health, as we discussed this week. Our spiritual heart pumps the blood of Christ through our bodies and enables us to live according to the will of God.

Our heart determines what we do for others. It enables us to hear from the Holy Spirit. It opens our minds to accept God's rebuke. It allows us to hear the voice of God and obey. Every action and reaction flows from our heart. These can either be good or bad experiences, and the outcome is dependent upon the condition of our heart.

Satan is the enemy of our heart. He is in a constant state of destruction. He throws everything in his arsenal at us to trip us up.

If you were going to be in battle against a real army, you would build a fortress to protect yourself. Look at the medieval knights. They built monstrous walls around their castles and stationed armed guards around the top of the walls. They constructed lookout towers with alarm bells to warn of impending danger. Their castles were, for the most part, impenetrable.

A little subterfuge

We can learn a lesson from the mythological story of the Trojan Horse.

The Greeks had spent a fruitless ten years trying to conquer the city of Troy. The city was well-fortified, and any attempts to break in had proven futile, so they devised a plan to have the people of Troy simply invite them in. Sounds crazy, but it worked. The Greeks constructed a huge hollow wooden horse and hid their soldiers inside of it. They then pretended to sail away, giving the people of Troy a false sense of security. The people opened their gates and pulled the horse inside, claiming victory.

That night, the Greek soldiers crept out of the horse and opened the gate for the rest of the army, which had returned after dark. The Greeks walked right in and destroyed the city of Troy, ending the war. The people of Troy brought about their own destruction.

Hacked

Modern day hackers use hidden malicious code (viruses) using the Trojan horse concept to wreak havoc on millions of unsuspecting computer owners. These modern day Trojans come in the form of useful or interesting articles which victims install on their computers. I'm sure you've been victimized at least once or twice in this manner. A tweet comes in, informing me the sender just saw a compromising video of me online. Just click this link … Ah, no thanks.

The frustrating thing about being hacked is realizing we invited it in. All our passwords and firewalls don't do a bit of good when we download the virus ourselves. We feel invincible with our Norton anti-virus program, and our 16-digit password made up of upper and lowercase letters and numbers, but in reality, are we safe from ourselves?

Satan's Trojan Horse

You pray. You go to church. You don't murder or rob people. You feel strong against the Devil. But he is not going to attack you where you expect it. Like hackers that post an interesting article wrapped around a virus, Satan uses people to create shows and movies that you find interesting and entertaining. Satan doesn't break down your walls. You invite him in. We go to the store and see the 60-inch flat screen Trojan horse, bring it home, and watch movies filled with all the things God detests. Fun, action-packed entertainment. It does not feel like sin. We install the virus right into our hearts and minds, and the enemy destroys us from the inside.

Like the soldiers that opened the gates for the rest of their army, Satan uses Hollywood to open the gate for other sins to manifest in our lives. Watching sexual scenes in movies can open the door to porn or watching profanity-laced movies can lead to cursing.

Scripture Minute

Finally brothers and sisters, whatever is true, whatever is noble, whatever is right, whatever is pure, whatever is lovely, whatever is admirable- if anything is excellent or praiseworthy-think about such things.

(Philippians 4:8, NIV)

I will not look with approval on anything vile.

(Psalm 101:3, NIV)

I made a covenant with my eyes not to look lustfully at a young woman.

(Job 31:1, NIV)

Rather, clothe yourselves with the Lord Jesus Christ, and do not think about how to gratify the desires of the flesh.

(Romans 13:14, NIV)

Spoiler Alert:
The horse is a trap
Don't open the gate

Week 7 Day 7

1) King Solomon warned us to guard our heart because everything we do flows from it. What are some things you can do to guard your heart against the enemy's attacks?

2) What steps can you take to ensure you have a peaceful heart?

3) We talked about loving God with all your heart, mind and strength. What does that look like lived out in your life?

4) We can talk about change all day long, but nothing changes until we do something. Talk is cheap without action, but extremely expensive. It costs us our reputation. How can you walk the talk?

5) We have established that TV can be bad for your spiritual heart, depending on what you watch. What are some things you can do that are good for your spiritual heart?

6) We exposed one Trojan horse this week, your TV. What are some other possible Trojan horses in your life? What can you do to uninstall some of the viruses they have downloaded in your life?

7) If Jesus came over to watch TV with you, what regular show would you have to skip?

8) In light of what you learned this week, what about *that* show do you think is a spiritual virus?

What Are You Feeding
Your Soul?

Week 8 Day 1

Comfort food

Meatloaf, mashed potatoes, and macaroni and cheese ... evil incarnate. Why do I declare these seemingly innocent food dishes evil? It's because they are what I turn to during times of stress and anxiety. They are warm, familiar, and inviting. They provide me with a false sense of comfort, and they wreak havoc on my plans to have abs of steel and a chest of iron.

Every time I start a diet, without fail, some sort of turmoil arises in my life. I'll start my diet like a boss—pumping iron, sweating through cardio, drinking gallons of water, eating lots of protein, and feeling the burn. Then, 20 minutes into my new diet and exercise program, I fly off the rails due to some stressful situation. I'm cruising along and then boom, a commercial for dark chocolate covered chocolatey chocolate balls cereal hits the market. I can't handle that kind of stress man, you feel me? I need a five-pound meatloaf *stat* and don't forget the side bucket of mashed potatoes. Do you have any hot buttered rolls?

Off and on

I take pounds off. I put pounds on. I take pounds off ... It becomes a vicious cycle. I do well and see improvement, but something sends or sucks me back to my old ways. It becomes, to me, a losing battle. Why try? I know the outcome already.

I'm not alone in feeling this way. Millions of people join gyms on January 2nd every year, with hopes of this being 'THE YEAR.' The gyms are packed solid all over the United States, but come the third week in January, we are talking Zombie apocalypse. The gyms are desolate arenas of failed dreams. The fitness fanatics get sidelined by life come week two and limp through week three, only to give up and say, "There's always next year."

What you know

It's easier to return to what you know than to continue into the unknown. My old life is right there where I left it, patiently waiting for my inevitable return. It's welcoming and familiar, and like mom's meatloaf, comforting.

I rationalize. I'm six-foot tall and 170 lbs. Not so bad. I tell myself I made it my whole life without Dwayne "The Rock" Johnson's muscles, so do I really need to be buff? I make lots of excuses and rationalizations for not following through. I look around at my friends, and none of them look like "The Rock" either. We are all ordinary, and I find solace in that. I lower my standards from "The Rock" to the standards of those around me.

I want to be in shape, but I don't want to do what it would take. I do not have the discipline to go the distance. Back to business as usual. Pass the macaroni and cheese, please.

When we turn from our old lives, we leave behind the familiar and head into unknown territory. You might be leaving behind friends who were part of your past but would only hinder your attempt to break free from your old life. You will miss them, but you need to move forward, and they will only hold you back.

You make new church friends. You start getting into this whole God thing, and it's pretty cool. People are nice. Everybody calls you brother and hugs feel great. You're meeting new friends over coffee. Yeah, life's good.

Cue the enemy

Boom, three weeks into your new life, the road gets rough. Maybe your girlfriend just ain't into this whole Jesus thing. Your family doesn't get it. The road ahead looks like an IED went off in the middle of it. You don't want to crawl through all the mess. Who knows how long these troubles will last? You look back, and suddenly, your old life looks like a nice big plate of meatloaf.

You start thinking about going back to the comfort food of your old life. There're friends back there you've known your whole life. They get you. Maybe you can still salvage your relationship with your girl. Going back to the familiar seems easier than going forward into the unknown.

But none of your friends are living for God, and instead of raising your standards to Jesus, you lower them to those around you.

Satan's meal plan

Satan wants to be your dietitian. He wants you to stay in your comfort zone, eating comfort food. His plan to accomplish this is extremely simple. He will send trials, persecution, troubles, stress, worries, fear, anger, even a dash of hate, and mix it all together in a big bowl with an egg, and some salt ... **BOOM!** You have got yourself a comfortable meatloaf.

He drizzles some guilt over the top of it to seal the deal. You turn back to your old life, feeling unworthy and realizing you don't have what it takes to live for God. Your old friends welcome you back with affirmation, "It's okay. We knew you'd be back. Let's go get a beer."

You are right

Right there, when you realized that you could not live for God, you were closer than you thought to successfully living for God. We are screw ups, but guess what? He already knew that. We need to surrender to God and admit we can't do it. Every second of every day, we are to live dependent on God in order to live for him.

We need a daily diet of Scripture intake. We need daily intake of the living water. We need to be in daily conversation with the Lord of our life. That's the only way we will successfully stay connected and persevere in our walk with God, the only way it will last a lifetime.

Psalms 119 gives us a blueprint for a successfully consistent lifetime walk with God:

I have hidden your word in my heart that I might not sin against you. Praise be to you, O LORD; teach me your decrees. With my lips recount all the laws that come from your mouth. I rejoice in following your statutes as one rejoices in great riches. I meditate on your precepts and consider your ways. I delight in your decrees; I will not neglect your word. (Psalm 119:11-16, NIV)

Satan knows you are a failure. He just wants you to think God is too. You will fail in your own power. Thankfully, God does not expect you to live in your own power. Don't eat Satan's lies.

Scripture Minute

*Brothers and sisters, I do not consider myself
yet to have taken hold of it.
But one thing I do: Forgetting what is behind
and straining toward what is ahead.*

(Philippians 3:13, NIV)

*Do not say, "Why were the old days better than these?"
For it is not wise to ask such questions.*

(Ecclesiastes 7:10, NIV)

*There is a way that appears to be right,
but in the end, leads to death.*

(Proverbs 14:12, NIV)

*I am the vine; you are the branches. If you remain in
me and I in you, you will bear much fruit;
apart from me you can do nothing.*

(John 15:5, NIV)

You can't out exercise a bad diet.

Week 8 Day 2

Living water

Your physical body needs water to survive. Many young people exist on Mountain Dew and Monster energy drinks, with very little water intake. Although there is water in these drinks, it's not enough to provide what your body needs.

If you continue to drink nothing but these carbonated drinks, you will eventually develop health problems. Since muscles require plenty of pure water for growth, you won't have to worry about having any. Your internal organs need pure water to function properly, so you will have issues with them as well. Bottom line, drinking plenty of pure water is essential to your health and survival.

Thirsty spirit

Like your physical body survives on pure water, your spirit survives on another type of pure water. Jesus made this fact very clear:

Jesus answered, "Everyone who drinks this water will be thirsty again, but whoever drinks the water I give them will never thirst. Indeed, the water I give them will become in them a spring of water welling up to eternal life." (John 4:13-14, NIV)

Jesus promised we could take one sip and never be thirsty again. It sounds crazy and too good to be true. So what exactly is this Living Water Jesus spoke of? For the answer, we need to look at John 7:37-39:

On the last and greatest day of the Feast, Jesus stood and said in a loud voice, "If anyone is thirsty, let him come to me and drink. Whoever believes in me, as the Scripture has said, streams of living water will flow from within him." By this he meant the Spirit, whom those who believed in him would receive. Up to that time the Spirit had not yet been given, since Jesus had not yet been glorified. (John 7:37-39, NIV)

Spirit provisions

His divine power, (Holy Spirit), has given us everything we need for life and godliness through our knowledge of him who called us by his own glory and goodness. Through these he has given us his very great and precious promises, so that through them you may participate in the divine nature and escape the corruption in the world caused by evil desires. (2 Peter 1:3,4, NIV)

The Power is available to us, but we have to put it into practice. Peter shares with us the secret of partaking in this Living Water.

For this very reason, make every effort to add to your faith goodness; and to goodness, knowledge; and to knowledge, self-control; and to self-control, perseverance; and to perseverance, godliness; and to godliness, brotherly kindness; and to brotherly kindness, love. For if you possess these qualities in increasing measure, they will keep you from being ineffective and unproductive in your knowledge of our Lord Jesus Christ. (2 Peter 1:5-8, NIV)

If you submerge yourself daily in the Word of God and put what you learn in the Word into practice, you will overcome trials and temptations. You will grow stronger in your faith and closer in your walk with God.

Scripture Minute

For this reason, since the day we heard about you, we have not stopped praying for you. We continually ask God to fill you with the knowledge of his will through all the wisdom and understanding that the Spirit gives.

(Colossians 1:9, NIV)

But grow in the grace and knowledge of our Lord and Savior Jesus Christ. To him be the glory both now and forever! Amen.

(2 Peter 3:18, NIV)

Blessed are those who hunger and thirst for righteousness, for they will be filled.

(Matthew 5:6, NIV)

Instead, speaking the truth in love, we will grow to become in every respect the mature body of him who is the head, that is, Christ.

(Ephesians 4:15-16, NIV)

Jump in. The Living Water is fine.

Week 8 Day 3

Litter Pan Theology

To say that I frequently have visitors over to my house would be an understatement. We literally have guests over every day. I like to have a clean, inviting home when friends arrive.

To maintain this standard, my wife and I clean the house every day. Every night when our visitors leave, we have games to put away, little ones to clean up after, toys to put away, dishes to wash, floors to sweep, carpets to vacuum ... the list goes on. All of this is in preparation for the next day's visitors.

What if I did all this cleaning but left my cat's dirty litter pan in the middle of my living room? What if I failed to empty it for weeks? What if I simply dusted the furniture and vacuumed around it? Would you notice my clean dining room? What if I invited you in and acted like the filthy, stinking, eye-watering litter pan was not even there?

You'd wonder why I was worried about dusting my knickknacks while ignoring the most obvious thing that needed to be dealt with. I could spend hours on "routine" maintenance issues around my house, but until I deal with that big pile of stinky cat poo, none of it will matter.

Many who profess to be Christ-following churchgoers practice Litter Pan Theology. They come to church each week, sing some songs, throw a few bucks in the offering, listen to a good sermon, and go home. Meanwhile, they have a major issue in their life they neglect, things only they know about. They play the game, do a few little religious things, and skirt the real issue. They dust around the edges, wash the windows, look around, and say, "Perfect!" All the while, they have this big crap-filled litter pan in the middle of their life and completely ignore it.

Dump the pan

What they need to do is dump the litter pan. Get rid of the steaming pile of crap. If they refuse to deal with this issue, they are wasting their time coming to church. A filthy litter pan overpowers everything else in your life. Just like a burning cat urine smell permeates everything in your home, a sin issue you refuse to deal with taints everything you do. You will be ineffective in your walk and in your ability to hear from God.

If you don't deal with the issue of sin, you put it ahead of God. Anything you put ahead of God becomes your god. Don't worship a litter pan.

Scripture Minute

He who conceals his sin does not prosper,
but whoever confesses and renounces them finds mercy.

(Proverbs 28:13, NIV)

If we confess our sins, he is faithful and just and will forgive us our
sins and purify us from all unrighteousness.

(1 John 1:9, NIV)

Therefore confess your sins to each other so that you may be healed.
The prayer of a righteous person is powerful and effective.

(James 5:16, NIV)

Then I acknowledged my sin to you and did not cover up my iniquity.
I said, "I will confess my transgressions to the LORD"-
and you forgave the guilt of my sin.

(Psalm 32:5, NIV)

Many of those who believed now came and
openly confessed what they had done.

(Acts 19:18, TNIV)

Make repentance part of your daily diet.

Week 8 Day 4

I don't want you to read your Bible

I want YOU to want to read your Bible. If you missed that, here it is again. I don't want you to read your Bible because I said so, I want you to want to read your Bible. I don't want you to pray. I want you to want to pray.

There's a big difference

I have adult children living in several different states. If they called me only because I wanted them to, it would be out of obligation. However, if they call me because they want to, that's love. Do you get that?

I work with at-risk teens, and I want them all to stay out of trouble, graduate, get a great job, and live a life of purpose. But me wanting that for them is not enough. They have to want it for themselves or it won't happen.

In my quest to fulfill Jesus' command to make disciples, not just churchgoers, I know these disciples will need to be in the Word of God daily and also communicating with God through daily prayer. They need to see the need for it. They need to be disciplined in their daily life, or they will never really be true disciples.

So how do I get people to want to read their Bibles and pray? It's simple. I don't. I simply connect them with the one who can.

For it is God who works in you to will and to act according to his good purpose. (Philippians 2:13, NIV)

Greater is He

God is at work in you, helping you want to obey him and then helping you do what he wants. As a Christian, you are no longer a slave sin because God has changed your 'want to.'

The closer you grow to God, the more you will want to read His Word and pray to Him. The more you do these things, the closer you will grow to Him.

Off base

When Jesus commanded us to go and make disciples, he had something completely different in mind than what we consider a disciple today.

Jesus would define a disciple as someone who surrendered his life and everything he had to the cause of Christ. He would take up his cross and follow in the footsteps of Jesus. He would imitate Christ in word and deed.

Admirers

I looked up the definition of admirer, and it seems a better fit for what we call those who recite a short prayer and go to church most Sundays. The modern day disciple.

Admirer: someone who has a particular regard for someone or something.

Jesus has a lot of secret admirers in churches all over America. They hold him in regard but at arm's length. They know of him like you know of your favorite actor or musician, but they don't intimately know him.

Change of Heart

When I look to make disciples, I'm seeking to help facilitate a change of heart in the person. To create a people who love God with all their heart, mind, soul, and strength.

I want to help them fall in love with their Savior, Jesus Christ.

I don't want them to read their Bible because they think they're supposed to. I want them to read it because they cannot get enough of it.

I want them to pray because it is their heart's desire to be in daily communion with God. This is my hope and prayer for you too, the reader, to experience this type of relationship with God and to help others become disciples with changed hearts.

This is how you will know you have created true disciples. This is how you will know if you are a true disciple of Christ.

Scripture Minute

Like newborn babies, crave pure spiritual milk, so that by it you may grow up in your salvation, now that you have tasted that the Lord is good.

(1 Peter 2:2, NIV)

"For the bread of God is the bread that comes down from heaven and gives life to the world." "Sir," they said, "always give us this bread." Then Jesus declared, "I am the bread of life. Whoever comes to me will never go hungry, and whoever believes in me will never be thirsty."

(John 6:33-35, TNIV)

You, God, are my God, earnestly I seek you; I thirst for you, my whole being longs for you, in a dry and parched land where there is no water.

(Psalm 63:1, TNIV)

I spread out my hands to you; I thirst for you like a parched land.

(Psalm 143:6, NIV)

My soul thirsts for God, for the living God. When can I go and meet with God?

(Psalm 42:2, NIV)

Go read your Bible because YOU want to.

Week 8 Day 5

Grab the pelican

Sometimes in my downtime, which is not often, I scroll through Facebook and watch crazy videos my friends post. I've watched countless stunts gone bad and adorable talking dog videos. Don't you judge me.

Yesterday, someone posted a video of a guy sneaking up on a pelican. Since this could not end well, I decided to watch. The guy grabbed the pelican by the foot as it tried to fly away. Let's just say the pelican was not thrilled with this and tried to beat the guy with it's wings. The guy straddled the pelican on the dock while others stood around watching.

For your own good

Another guy came in and grabbed the pelican by the bill. I couldn't understand why these guys were trying to harm this poor pelican.

Then it became clear. A fishing net had become tangled around its bill, trapping it shut. The pelican could not eat. These "terrible" men were actually heroes trying to save the bird, only no one told the pelican. He put up a fight the whole time, making it very difficult for the guys to help him. After several minutes of struggling, the two guys cut the net off, and the pelican was free. It did not stick around to say thanks but instead, shot off like a rocket.

Thanks Mom

When the video ended, I immediately thought of a few times I've been just like that pelican. No, I never got my mouth stuck shut in a net, but I have fought against God when He was holding me down, trying to save me from something harmful.

Oblivious to God's efforts to help me through discipline, like the pelican, I fight it the whole time. Discipline never feels good at the time, I'm sure you agree. My mom would always say, "You'll thank me later." I'd be like, "Yeah right, NOT."

The crazy part is, she was right. Things have come full circle, and I find myself saying the same thing to my kids when I discipline them. And you'll say the same thing to your kids someday.

No pain No peace

The Apostle Paul nailed it when he wrote on the topic of discipline.

No discipline seems pleasant at the time, but painful. Later on, however, it produces a harvest of righteousness and peace for those who have been trained by it. (Hebrew 12:11, NIV)

We need to embrace discipline as part of our spiritual training. God disciplines those he loves. Just like I discipline my children because I love them and want the best for them.

Scripture Minute

My son, do not despise the LORD's discipline and do not resent his rebuke, because the LORD disciplines those he loves, as a father the son he delights in.

(Proverbs 3:11-12, NIV)

A fool spurns his father's discipline, but whoever heeds correction shows prudence.

(Proverbs 15:5, NIV)

The next time God grabs you
but the foot, don't try to fly away.

Week 8 Day 6

Day One

One of my favorite songs is *Day One* by Matthew West. You need to check it out. But the point of the song is this: Yesterday is gone, Today is Day One of the rest of your life. As we come to the end of this journey together, I wanted to leave you with some profound words.

Yesterday does not matter. You can't relive it. You can't change it. Good or bad, it's gone. Today is all you have, so make it count. Do something great. Start right where you are.

Do you have a strained relationship with your parents? Go apologize for your part. Bad grades in school? Start over and study. Apply yourself. Have not read your Bible in a while? Begin again today. Stuck on a mission in that video game? Start over.

Follow the signs

I go on a lot of road trips. And when I do, I follow the big green directional signs along the highway ahead of me. These signs allow me to continue in the right direction.

I never look out the back window at the signs on the other side of the highway. It does me no good to focus on where I've been. Plus, it would be extremely dangerous with deadly results.

Words of Wisdom

The Bible has a few things to say on the subject as well.

Forget the former things; do not dwell on the past. (Isaiah 43:18, NIV)
Brothers and sisters, I do not consider myself yet to have taken hold of it. But one thing I do: Forgetting what is behind and straining toward what is ahead, I press on toward the goal to win the prize for which God has called me heavenward in Christ Jesus (Philippians 3:13-14, TNIV).

86400

That's how many seconds you get every day. 3600 every hour, 24 hours a day. That's a lot of seconds, and they slip away quickly. Use them wisely.

Today, you could impact someone's life for eternity. You could feed someone a meal. You could visit a lonely senior. Pray for a sick person. Babysit for a single parent. Make cookies for your bus driver. Help your brother with his homework. Write your parents a note. Call your grandmother. Mow a neighbor's lawn. Read your Bible. Write your testimony. You can do all this, a little, every day. Start.

Scripture Minute

Be wise in the way you act towards outsiders;
make the most of every opportunity.

(Colossians 4:5, NIV)

In the same way, let your light shine before others,
that they may see your good deeds and glorify your Father in heaven.

(Matthew 5:16, TNIV)

Make today count. You may not get another.

Week 8 Day 7

On this, our last day together, I want to leave you with practical things you can do to make a difference in the lives of those around you. It is my hope and prayer that you take these things to heart and that you find yourself more blessed than those you bless.

Hebrews 13:16 *And do not forget to do good and to share with others, for with such sacrifices God is pleased* (NIV).

What good thing can you share with others to make a positive impact in their life? Maybe your time. Maybe a sympathetic ear? Homework help?

Luke 3:11 *John answered, "Anyone who has two shirts should share with the one who has none, and anyone who has food should do the same.* (TNIV)

Could you give away some of the clothes you don't wear? Could you give an extra pair of shoes to someone? Maybe you and some friends could organize a food drive or coat drive.

Romans 12:13 *Share with the Lord's people who are in need. Practice hospitality.* (TNIV)

Maybe you could take a meal to a family that just had a baby or just got out of the hospital. You could visit a senior center and spend time with the elderly residents there.

Hebrews 10:24 *And let us consider how we may spur one another on toward love and good deeds.* (NIV)

Who are some people you could encourage to join you in making a difference in your community?

1 Thessalonians 5:11 *Therefore encourage one another and build each other up, just as in fact you are doing.* (NIV)

Make a list of some friends you could invite to church or the next youth event at your church. Invite one of the teens considered "unpopular" at your school to join you for coffee at a cafe. Listen to them. Get to know them.

Galatians 6:2 *Carry each other's burdens, and in this way you will fulfill the law of Christ.* (NIV)

Find some people who are lonely, hurting, or depressed and spend some quality time with them. Give them an outlet for their grief. Be a shoulder to lean or cry on.

Mark 16:15 *"Go into all the world and preach the gospel to all creation."* (TNIV)

This is the most important thing you can and need to be doing. But remember, evangelism is something you live, not something you do. Live out your faith and let your light shine in a dark world.

Thank you for spending this time with me. I hope you enjoyed reading this book as much as I did writing it. It drew me even closer to God as I researched all the scriptures I included. Some of the scriptures, as you probably noticed, appeared more than once. This was intentional as I wanted you to start to memorize them.

I hope you marked this copy up, and I pray you share it with your friends.

My personal email is rcook252underground@gmail.com Feel free to shoot me an email with any questions or comments.

My author web-site is www.robcookunderground.com

You can also check out my Blog at www.regener8ted.com

If you have not already read my book REGENER8, you can grab a copy on Amazon.com

I prayed for you as I wrote this book. I prayed the Holy Spirit would do something mighty in your life. I prayed you would turn the world upside down.

Remember, you are never alone. God is with you even in the times you think he is not. Well, I got to get started on my next book, ACTIV8. See you soon.

**What will you do
with your
24?**